SCIENTIFIC BREAKTHROUGHS

Philosophy, Invention, and Engineering

TEACHER RESOURCES

Edited by Tim Cooke

LIGHTBOX
openlightbox.com

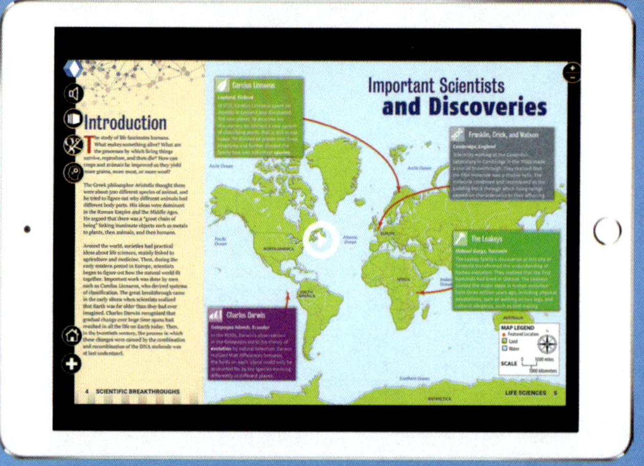

Lightbox is an all-inclusive digital solution for the teaching and learning of curriculum topics in an original, groundbreaking way. Lightbox is based on National Curriculum Standards.

STANDARD FEATURES OF LIGHTBOX

 **AUDIO** High-quality narration using text-to-speech system

 **VIDEOS** Embedded high-definition video clips

ACTIVITIES Printable PDFs that can be emailed and graded

 **WEBLINKS** Curated links to external, child-safe resources

  **SLIDESHOWS** Pictorial overviews of key concepts

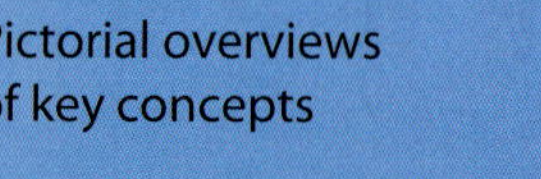 **TRANSPARENCIES** Step-by-step layering of maps, diagrams, charts, and timelines

 **INTERACTIVE MAPS** Interactive maps and aerial satellite imagery

QUIZZES Ten multiple choice questions that are automatically graded and emailed for teacher assessment

 **KEY WORDS** Matching key concepts to their definitions

 **MORE** Extra information and details on the subject

 **FIRST HAND** Letters, diaries, and other primary sources

 **DOCS** Speeches, newspaper articles, and other historical documents

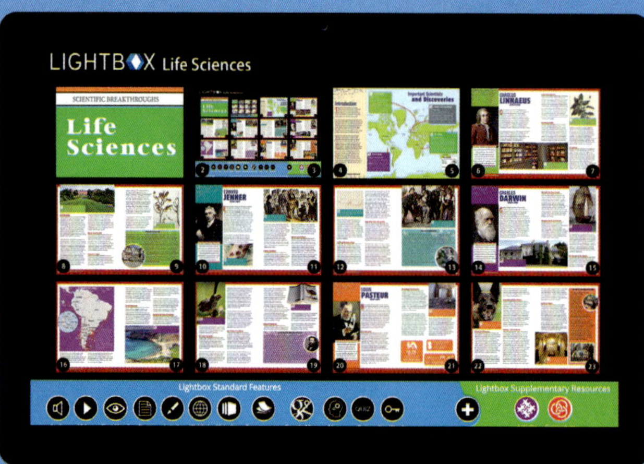

Contents

RUBRIC

Conducting an Interview

Students will conduct an interview with a member of the scientific community about a significant discovery he or she made or important research he or she conducted. The student is to submit an audio recording and transcript of the interview. An exemplary interview will meet the following criteria.

- Clearly defines the purpose of the interview
- Conducts thorough background research to inform the focus of the interview and the questions
- Drafts a complete list of thoughtful, in-depth, and varied questions prior to the interview
- Interviews a subject with relevant knowledge on the topic and time period in question
- Asks questions in a logical order, building upon each other
- Treats the interview subject in a polite and professional manner
- Does not interrupt or rush the interview subject
- Shows interest and enthusiasm in responses and follow-up questions
- Chooses follow-up questions that demonstrate active listening
- Asks for clarification and further details when necessary
- Asks questions about personal experiences related to the topic
- Asks questions regarding factual information and the interview subject's opinion on the topic
- Asks creative questions that reflect fresh insights on the topic
- Records the full interview in a quiet environment
- Organizes and edits the interview transcript to be clear and factual

Introduction

Throughout most of history, there was little difference between philosophy and science. Philosophers, such as the ancient Greeks Plato and Aristotle, were trying to understand and explain the nature of the world around them. They observed natural phenomena closely in order to make logical deductions that would apply universally. Much later, in the seventeenth and eighteenth centuries, the people who made the first modern scientific analysis of the natural world were still known as natural philosophers.

Many of these natural philosophers did not simply want to understand the world. They wanted to be able to improve it by devising machines that would make human tasks easier. During the 1700s, understanding of water and steam led to the evolution of the steam engine. This revolutionized work and society, starting the Industrial Revolution.

The late 1800s saw a period of intense invention have a huge impact on the nature of communications, transportation, and daily life. The rapid pace of change continued in the twentieth century, with huge advances in chemical engineering, medicine and public health, and, ultimately, the development and spread of the computer. By 2000, the computer had become the basis for much modern life.

James Watt

Birmingham, United Kingdom

Born in Scotland, engineer James Watt later moved to the city of Birmingham in the English Midlands. The city was home to the factory of the ironmaker Matthew Boulton. The two men formed a company to manufacture the steam engines Watt had invented in 1765. At that time, he improved the design that had been in operation for about 50 years. He later went on to make further improvements to the steam engine.

Thomas A. Edison

Menlo Park, New Jersey

In 1876, Thomas Alva Edison set up a workshop and laboratory at Menlo Park to develop his own inventions. He invented both the phonograph and the incandescent light bulb there. Edison went on to become one of the most prolific and influential inventors in history.

Important Scientists and Discoveries

Alan Turing

Bletchley Park, United Kingdom

A talented mathematician, Alan Turing led the top-secret British attempt to crack German military codes during World War II (1939–1945). He devised the first practical computers for the purpose. He also predicted the rise of computer use and the emergence of **artificial intelligence**, or AI.

Aristotle

Athens, Greece

After studying with the philosopher Plato in Athens as a young man, Aristotle later opened his own school in the city in 335 BC. He thought deeply about a range of subjects and had insights about logic and animal classification. He also tried to figure out the laws of **motion** on Earth and in the heavens.

EXTENSION ACTIVITY

Google Maps

Important Scientists and Discoveries

Explore these locations using street view to learn more about important scientists and their discoveries.

1. What do these locations have in common with each other? What are the differences between them?
2. Why are these discoveries associated with these specific locations? In your opinion, would the work of these scientists and their discoveries have been possible elsewhere? Support your opinions with examples.

ARISTOTLE

384 BC–322 BC

The ancient Greek philosopher Aristotle spanned all branches of human knowledge. He studied subjects from zoology to politics. He also made a lasting impact on the thoughts and scientific discoveries of later civilizations.

Aristotle was born in 384 BC in Stagira, in Greece. In 367 BC, he went to study at the Academy in Athens, founded by the philosopher Plato. Aristotle stayed there for 20 years, after which he went to Assos, on the coast of what is now northwest Turkey. Here, he befriended another philosopher, Theophrastus, with whom he moved to Mytilene, the chief city on the island of Lesbos. Aristotle studied the island's natural history. In 342 BC, he returned to Macedonia to teach the Macedonian king Philip II's 14-year-old son, Alexander. After King Philip II's death, Aristotle's royal pupil would conquer most of the known world as Alexander the Great. In about 339 BC, Aristotle returned to Stagira, where he continued to record as much as he could about the natural world.

Aristotle returned to Athens in 335 BC and founded his own school, called the Lyceum. After Alexander's death in 323 BC, there was an outbreak of anti-Macedonian sentiment in Athens. Aristotle seems to have felt threatened by it, and he retired to the island of Euboea, where he died soon afterward, in 322 BC. Theophrastus succeeded him as head of the Lyceum in Athens.

Early Scientific Beliefs

The ancient Greeks were artistic, literate, and educated, and science and philosophy had been studied from long before Aristotle's time. The founder of Greek science and philosophy was traditionally believed to be Thales of Miletus, who lived in the sixth century BC. Thales had declared that he believed everything was made of water.

This was probably because he was able to observe that liquid water is transformed into air as steam and into a solid as ice. Other Greek scientists believed that all natural objects are made from four basic elements, namely earth, air, water, and fire. Others argued that the world is made up of indivisible units of matter the Greeks called atoms.

At the Lyceum, Aristotle and his students debated different sides of an argument to try to establish what was true about the world.

Greek thought was highly **rational**. Ideas were reached by systematically collecting all the known facts about a subject and placing them within an overall scheme. The high value given to literacy meant that ideas could be written down and passed around for general criticism and discussion.

Looking at Aristotle's Work

Many of Aristotle's ideas exist in the form of lecture notes or texts for students. Unlike modern scientists, Aristotle and his contemporaries did not use scientific experiments to confirm their theories. Aristotle always tried to support his ideas with evidence, however, based on his own observations and practical experience.

Aristotle was the first person to prove scientifically that Earth is shaped like a ball by observing that the shadow of Earth is round when it falls on the Moon during an **eclipse**. Like most thinkers of his day, Aristotle believed that Earth lay at the center of the universe. He believed that the **stars** and **planets** were carried on transparent spheres. According to Aristotle, the spheres rotated daily around a stationary Earth with steady circular motion but at different speeds. Beyond them, an additional sphere held the fixed stars. Not all Greek thinkers agreed. Aristarchus of Samos, for example, believed that the Sun, not Earth, lay at the center of the universe. But Aristotle's system became generally accepted and was to dominate European thought until the fifteenth century.

Aristotle also studied motion, beginning with the theory that "Whatever is moved is moved by something." This belief influenced scientists until the studies of Galileo Galilei and Isaac Newton in the 1600s. Even in Aristotle's time, the belief had its limitations, as people could see that, for example, apples fall to the ground from trees unaided. Aristotle defined three types of motion occurring on Earth. Living creatures move because they choose to, which he called "voluntary" motion. He called the second kind of motion "natural."

EXTENSION ACTIVITY

More

Schools in Ancient Greece/ Aristotle and Biology

Review the origins and evolution of schools in Ancient Greece.

1. How do Ancient Greek schools differ from contemporary education systems? In what ways are they the same? Support your answers with examples.
2. In your opinion, why were girls excluded from education? Think of other examples of discrimination in the educational environment in different historical periods. Why might they persist today?

Weblink

How Thales of Miletus Changed the World

Examine the life and achievements of Thales of Miletus.

1. In your opinion, what does the author mean by saying that Thales of Miletus "changed the world"? Justify your answer.
2. Describe Thales's water theory in your own words. Why did Thales consider water as the origin of all things? What does Thales's theory have in common with other scientific theories formulated in different historical periods?

Greek men met often to eat, listen to poetry, and discuss important questions. Women did not take part in such discussions.

Aristotle argued that objects were composed of only four elements, meaning earth, water, air, and fire. Earth, the heaviest element, lay at the center of the cosmos, surrounded by water, then air, then fire. When moved from their natural place, objects try to return to it. This explained why air bubbles rise through water, or why earth falls through air.

Aristotle noted that objects speed up as they fall. He thought this was because the nearer they got to their natural place, the greater the **force** attracting them. He wrongly believed that heavy objects fall faster than lighter ones, reasoning that the more matter an object contains, the more quickly it returns to its natural place. According to Aristotle's theory, an object such as an arrow would fall to the ground as soon as the "mover," meaning the archer, sets it in motion. This clearly did not happen, so Aristotle concluded that the medium that the object was passing through, which in this case was air, must somehow exert a force to move the object. He called the third type "violent" motion.

Nature of the Heavens

Aristotle believed that heavenly bodies, such as the stars and planets, moved in a circular motion unlike any type of motion on Earth. From this, he reasoned that the stars and planets are not subject to the laws that control the behavior of objects on Earth. Therefore, heavenly bodies could not be composed of the four elements but must be made of a fifth, different, element. Later philosophers came to call this fifth element quintessence, from *quinta*,which is Latin for fifth, and *essentia*, meaning the being or essence of a thing. Aristotle divided the heavens, or what is now called space, into two separate and distinct realms. These were the "superlunary," meaning above the Moon, and the "sublunary," meaning below the Moon.

Aristotle believed that the sublunary realm was subject to the same physical and natural laws that operate on Earth, but the superlunary realm was governed by its own laws. He believed that the Earthly elements change their form by losing one of a pair of opposite properties, known as "contraries," and gaining the other. Quintessence does not possess these contraries, however. Aristotle believed that there can be no change without contraries, so he concluded that the superlunary heavens must be unchangeable. From this, he reasoned that any object moving in the skies, such as a **comet** or lightning, must be part of the sublunary realm.

The teachings of Aristotle became popular in Europe in the Middle Ages, after they were rediscovered from copies of his works preserved in the Islamic world.

ARISTOTLE AND LOGIC

The term "logic" comes from the Greek word *logos*, meaning speech or reasoning. It was first used by Xenocrates in the fourth century BC, but it was Aristotle who provided some of the earliest surviving and complete texts on the subject. Aspects of Aristotelian logic are still taught today. One of the most famous examples of Aristotle's logic is called the "Aristotelian syllogistic." A syllogism is an argument based on deductive reasoning. A syllogism must have two premises, or assumptions, from which a person can draw a conclusion. For example:

All birds are two-legged
All eagles are birds
All eagles are two-legged

The first statement is the "major" premise, the second is the "minor" premise, and the last line draws a conclusion. The premises can be universal, so they refer to "all" or "no," or particular, when they refer to "some." They must be either affirmative, such as saying "All As are B", or negative, as in "No As are B." They must have a sign of quantity, such as "all." They must also contain three terms. These are major, in this case, "two-legged", minor, which is "eagles," and middle, which here is "birds."

A wrongly constructed syllogism can result in a logically flawed argument or fallacy. An example is, All birds can fly. Helicopters can fly. Therefore, helicopters are birds.

EXTENSION ACTIVITY

Document

Lives of the Eminent Philosophers
Analyze the excerpt from Diogenes Laërtius's *Lives of the Eminent Philosophers* about the life of Aristotle.

1. Extend your learning by researching the author of this text. Did he know Aristotle in person? Do you consider him to be a reliable source? Why or why not?
2. How does the author describe the life and scientific theories of Aristotle? Why are they described in these terms? Why, in your opinion, does the author present a lengthy list of Aristotle's work? Justify your answer.

Weblink

The End of Europe's Middle Ages: Intellectual Life
Examine the article discussing the reception of Aristotelian theories in the Middle Ages.

1. Why was Aristotle considered an "authority" during the Middle Ages? Formulate some hypotheses.
2. In your opinion, why was Aristotle's cosmology taught across Europe despite its conflict with Christian teachings? How did medieval scholars attempt to resolve this conflict?

JAMES WATT

1736–1819

James Watt improved the design of the first steam engine, built in 1712 by English inventor Thomas Newcomen. The steam engine became a vital part of the Industrial Revolution, which started in Britain in the late 1700s and spread to continental Europe and the United States.

James Watt was born on January 19, 1736, in Greenock, Scotland. He was a sickly child, so he did not go to school. Instead, his mother taught him at home. Watt was bright and inquisitive and spent hours taking his toys apart and putting them back together again. Watt failed to do well when he attended the local grammar school, and it was only at the age of 13 that his ability began to emerge, when he was introduced to **mathematics**. At home, he spent his spare time building models. He also developed an interest in ships' instruments.

At the age of 17, Watt decided to become an instrument-maker, or maker of scientific devices, and in 1755, he traveled to London to begin learning the trade. He returned to Scotland in 1757, where he set up a business in Glasgow making and repairing instruments, including compasses and weighing scales. One of his duties was to make mathematical instruments for Glasgow University.

In 1764, Watt was asked to repair a model of a steam engine invented by the English engineer Thomas Newcomen. He soon spotted a problem with Newcomen's basic design. Steam was being wasted because the cylinder was losing too much heat through the walls as the steam cooled and the piston returned to its original position. The engine came quickly to a stop. Watt decided he could improve the efficiency of the Newcomen engine by introducing a second chamber in which the steam could be **condensed**. This would allow the working cylinder that held the piston to keep its heat throughout the process.

Harnessing the Power of Air

Watt's engine was the culmination of centuries of experimentation. In the ancient world, people used air to perform various tasks, even if they were not aware of it. Suction pumps had been used since Roman times to raise water, for example. It took the seventeenth-century Italian physicist Evangelista Torricelli to explain how such pumps worked. Suction pumps comprise a cylinder enclosing a piston. When the piston is raised, a partial vacuum is created, and **atmospheric** pressure pushes water into the cylinder. The water then escapes through an outlet and the process is repeated. Such pumps could lift water no higher than 32 feet (9.75 meters). In order to raise water higher, two or more pumps are needed on successive levels.

James Watt was said to have started thinking about the power of steam as a young man after watching a kettle boil on a fire.

Torricelli showed that the weight of the atmosphere and the weight of the water in the cylinder are in balance at this height. The water cannot be lifted any higher. He predicted that, if the atmosphere had to balance a heavier liquid, the liquid would reach a much lower height. This was confirmed in 1643 by Italian scientist Vincenzo Viviani. He showed that mercury, which is 14 times heavier than water, would stand 14 times lower. It was clear that the atmosphere had power.

75 percent The amount of fuel James Watt's **new steam engine** saved compared to previous engines

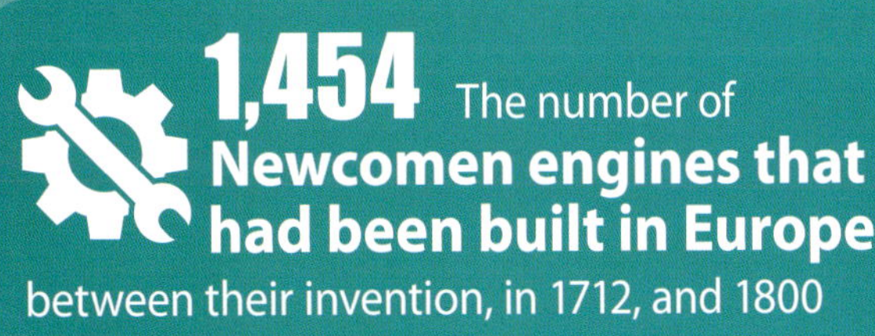

1,454 The number of **Newcomen engines that had been built in Europe** between their invention, in 1712, and 1800

11,200 horsepower The total power produced **by all 496 Watt steam engines** built by 1800

EXTENSION ACTIVITY

More

An Early Fascination

Examine the anecdote about James Watt.

1. Who is the source of the anecdote? Do you think the source is reliable? Why or why not?
2. What does this anecdote tell us about James Watt? Why did James Watt's aunt not understand what he was doing? Formulate some hypotheses.
3. Imagine this anecdote retold from the perspective of another inventor. How might this perspective compare to that of Watt's aunt?

Video

Newcomen Steam Engine

Assess the consequences of Newcomen's invention.

1. What was the function of steam in Newcomen's engine? What were the dangers of the first engine models? How did Newcomen eliminate these dangers?
2. Why was Newcomen's engine invented in this specific historical period and not earlier? Compare and contrast some possible reasons.

Using a vacuum pump to remove the air from between two metal hemispheres left them fastened tightly together thanks to the surrounding air pressure.

In 1650, the German engineer and physicist Otto von Guericke joined together two large copper hemispheres and pumped out the air inside them to create a vacuum. Von Guericke then arranged for two teams of eight horses to try to pull the hemispheres apart. They failed. This was because there was no pressure inside the hemispheres. The only force acting on them was the external weight, or pressure, of the atmosphere. When air reentered the hemispheres, they fell apart by themselves.

Watt Develops his Steam Engine

To develop his engine commercially, Watt needed financing and access to a big engineering works. In 1768, he entered into partnership with John Roebuck, the owner of an ironworks. The following year, Watt took out a patent for his new steam engine. A patent is a license that allows an inventor to be the only person to make, use, and sell his or her invention for a set length of time. Watt's patent was for "A New Invented Method of Lessening the Consumption of Steam and Fuel in Fire Engines."

In 1773, Roebuck went bankrupt and sold his interest in Watt's engine to Matthew Boulton, the owner of a manufacturing business in Birmingham. Boulton could see the great opportunities for trade in the Industrial Revolution that was beginning in England. Watt's partnership with Boulton lasted 25 years and gave him the financial backing to develop his engine.

Watt's patent was extended by the British government. From 1776, many of his engines were installed to pump water from mines, particularly in the copper and tin mines of Cornwall. Boulton began to encourage Watt to replace the action of the original machine, which used an up-and-down motion known to engineers as "reciprocating."

With this type of motion, **energy** is used first to accelerate the piston and then to stop it. As any cyclist knows, this wastes energy. Much less effort is needed to keep a bicycle moving forward at a steady speed by turning one's legs in a circular, or rotary, motion than to get it moving after a stop by pumping one's legs up and down. The simplest way to produce rotary motion is by using a crank, such as those used in modern car engines. The crank converts the reciprocating motion of the cylinders into circular motion at the drive shaft and then the wheels. Unfortunately for Watt, however, a patent on the crank had already been awarded in 1780 to another inventor. Instead of using a crank, Watt created other linking devices, including the sun-and-planet gear wheel, which transformed up-and-down motion into rotary motion.

Improving the Engine

In Watt's original design for his steam engine, steam operated on one side of the piston only. In 1782, Watt patented a method to allow steam to be admitted and condensed on both sides of the piston. This doubled the engine's output by producing power on both the up and the down strokes of the piston. The engine needed a new method of securing the piston to the beam. Watt solved the problem with an arrangement of rods that he described as "one of the most ingenious, simple pieces of mechanism I have contrived."

In 1794, Watt and Boulton set up the firm of Boulton & Watt and built a factory for making steam engines more efficiently. Watt's patents were due to run out in 1800, after which, other people could build steam engines, so he wanted to be ready to face the inevitable competition.

By 1800, Boulton and Watt's company had built about 500 engines. Most of them were of the rotary motion type. The engines soon became used by a range of industries.

High-Pressure Engines

Watt's engines, which worked at low temperatures and with low steam pressures, were large and cumbersome. Using higher steam pressure, which could be produced at greater temperatures, would raise the energy efficiency of the engine, but Watt thought that such engines were dangerous and that the higher pressures would bring an increased risk of explosions. He refused to work on the development of high-pressure engines.

When a furnace heated steam in a vertical cylinder, the up-and-down motion of the piston was able to raise and lower one end of a rocking beam.

EXTENSION ACTIVITY

More

The Atmospheric Engine

Analyze the development of Newcomen steam engine.

1. How did Newcomen's steam engine work? Describe its function in your own words.
2. In your opinion, how did Newcomen's profession influence the development of his invention? Justify your answers.
3. How did James Watt improve on Newcomen's design? In your opinion, do patents help or hinder technological advancements? Defend your responses with evidence.

First Hand

Letter from Erasmus Darwin to James Watt

Examine Erasmus Darwin's letter to James Watt written on March 29, 1775.

1. What were the potential advantages of extending Watt's patent? Formulate some theories.
2. Besides personal affection, what could have motivated Erasmus Darwin's opposition to James Watt moving to Russia?
3. How does Darwin describe James Watt's machines in the letter? Why?
4. Which books does Darwin expect Watt to procure for him? What do these titles tell us about the spread of scientific knowledge in the late eighteenth century?

RUBRIC

Answer a Scientific Question

Students will define a scientific question or problem, and carry out an investigation or experiment to answer it, then write a report on their findings. An exemplary report will meet the following criteria.

- Problem is written in the form of a question with a question mark at the end
- Hypothesis is written as a guess or explanation to the answer of the problem
- Hypothesis is written in a complete sentence (for example, "I think …," "I hypothesize …," "If…, then…")
- Variable and controls are clearly identified
- Procedure steps are in numbered order
- Procedure steps show what to measure and where to record the data
- Procedure steps are written in complete sentences
- Data is organized in a data table
- The investigation or experiment includes more then one trial
- All numbers have labels
- All calculations are complete
- Conclusion is written in complete sentences
- Conclusion states whether the hypothesis was right or wrong
- Conclusion answers the question written in the problem

James Watt made a series of improvements to the design of the steam engine, which became more efficient and more adaptable.

The terms of Watt's steam-engine patent were so broad that no one else could develop high-pressure engines either. Watt's opposition prevented other inventors from developing an improved steam engine for about 20 years. The first man to do so was the English inventor Richard Trevithick.

Trevithick was an enthusiast for high-pressure engines. In 1801, after Watt's patent ran out, Trevithick built his first steam carriage, which he drove up a hill in Cornwall. In 1802, he took out a patent for high-pressure engines for stationary and locomotive use. Trevithick had developed an ingenious safety measure against explosions. A safety valve on the boiler did not always guarantee protection because workers often screwed the valves down to make the machines easier to operate. This increased the risk of an explosion. Trevithick's answer was to use lead rivets in the boiler. The lead melted when the water reached a certain temperature, allowing steam to escape before an explosion could occur.

Watt's engines had huge cylinders up to 7 feet (2 m) in diameter. They were far too unwieldy to be used for transportation. The advantage of Trevithick's high-pressure engine was that it was smaller, lighter, and more efficient in fuel and energy. By 1804, Trevithick had built the first steam-powered locomotive. He used the vehicle to haul a load of iron and 70 men a distance of 10 miles (16 kilometers).

Trevithick was a talented engineer who made many improvements to boiler design and construction. Although his high-pressure engine was to prove highly versatile, it brought him no financial profit. Trevithick's lack of business sense was in marked contrast to Watt, who made a considerable amount of money from his invention. However, Watt was forced to spend time and money in court to defend his patents.

Calculating Payments

Watt's engines were first used in coal mines and ironworks. Boulton & Watt designed and supervised the building of the engine, while the customer paid the material and building costs. Profits were calculated on how much fuel the company's clients saved by installing one of their machines. A different method of payment was devised for the rotary engine, which operated mills of various kinds. Watt worked out that a horse, the previous source of mill power, could raise 33,000 pounds (14,969 kilograms) by one foot (30 centimeters) in one minute. He called this measure a horsepower, or hp. Mill owners paid a charge based on how many horsepower per year were provided by Watt's rotary engines. Horsepower is still used as a unit of work today.

In Retirement

Watt was married twice. His first marriage was to his cousin, Margaret Miller, with whom he had six children. After Margaret's death, he married Ann MacGregor, with whom he had two more children. He had a wide interest in instrument-making and scientific invention. When he retired in 1800, he turned the attic of his home into a workshop. He died there on August 25, 1819, aged 83.

The development of smaller high-pressure engines led to the building of steam trains in the early 1800s, which had a profound effect on U.S. settlement.

RICHARD TREVITHICK

Richard Trevithick taught himself engineering. Between 1801 and 1815, he built steam road carriages, stationary steam engines, and the world's first steam railroad locomotive. He also invented the Cornish pumping engine, which soon replaced Watt's machines. In 1816, Trevithick traveled to South America to sell his engines. While there, he fished for pearls, prospected for minerals, and fought in the wars of liberation alongside the revolutionary leader Simón Bolívar. Eventually, Trevithick returned to England, where he died, penniless.

EXTENSION ACTIVITY

Document

1781 Specification of Patent

Examine the patent specifications Watt wrote to complete his 1781 patent for his steam engine.

1. What is the function of the patent specifications? To what exactly do they refer? Why must they be so specific?
2. What do the drawings represent? In your opinion, why do the specifications contain drawings? Discuss some possible reasons.
3. Imagine Watt was an inventor today. How else might he communicate the specifications for his patent?

Weblink

Richard Trevithick's steam locomotive

Discover more about Richard Trevithick's locomotive invention and its first trip.

1. What did Trevithick record about the first trip of his locomotive? Why did he record specifically that information? Justify your answer.
2. What prompted Trevithick to work on this first locomotive? What problems did it encounter during its first trip? Why were these problems encountered? Why does a museum preserve a copy of this locomotive today?
3. Why is Trevithick described as the "real father of the railways"?
4. How did Trevithick's business success compare with his success as an inventor? Propose some possible reasons.

CHARLES **BABBAGE** & ADA **LOVELACE**

(Babbage) 1791–1871, (Lovelace) 1815–1852

Charles Babbage was born on December 26, 1791, in England. He attended several schools but was home tutored in the subject he liked best, math. In 1810, he entered Cambridge University. In 1812, while at Cambridge, Babbage and the English astronomer John Herschel helped form the Analytical Society, which aimed to introduce modern mathematical methods to the university. The problem lay with the calculus. This was the branch of mathematics discovered by English scientist Sir Isaac Newton and German philosopher and mathematician Gottfried Leibniz.

Charles Babbage realized that the regular relations between numbers meant that he could carry out computations by building what he called a difference engine.

Charles Babbage, an English mathematician, believed it was possible to create a machine that could store information and work from a set of instructions. His ideas influenced the modern computer revolution. Ada Lovelace created the first computer program for him.

Whereas the signs and symbols used by mathematicians in continental Europe were based on those developed by Leibniz, most British scientists followed Newton's method. However, Newton's system was more cumbersome than Leibniz's, and the development of the calculus in Britain lagged behind continental Europe. Babbage, who had learned Leibniz's system, wanted others to do the same.

Simplifying Calculations

Since ancient times, people have tried various methods to simplify calculations. One of the earliest devices, the abacus, is still in use in many parts of the world. It usually consists of rows of movable beads strung on rods or wires within a frame. In addition to the calculus, another important aid to calculation, known as logarithms, was invented in 1614 by John Napier, a Scottish mathematician. In 1642 to 1644, French philosopher Blaise Pascal invented the first digital calculating machine. The design was later refined by Leibniz.

In 1819, Babbage began to think about how to use mechanical methods to undertake more advanced mathematical calculations. He was inspired by a passage in the *Wealth of Nations* by the Scottish economist Adam Smith. Smith pointed out that if one man working alone had to manufacture pins, he would find it difficult to finish one pin a day. If each employee carried out just one part of the process, though, it would speed it up greatly. Smith reported that he had seen a factory of 10 men produce 48,000 pins a day.

Babbage wondered if Smith's approach could be applied to calculation. He saw a link with the work of the French mathematician François de Prony. The metric system had been introduced in France in the 1790s.

Scottish mathematician John Napier devised a way to speed up calculations using a set of rods marked with numbers. The rods were known as "Napier's bones.".

To prepare the new mathematical tables needed to serve the metric system, de Prony organized his workers on an assembly line, with each worker performing simple additions or subtractions. The labor was divided into easy, repeated operations, and Babbage decided that the workers were acting "mechanically." He thought he could replace workers with a calculating machine.

The Difference Engine

Babbage set out to build a machine based on the "method of differences." He constructed a table of cubes, or numbers that have been multiplied by themselves three times. Babbage figured out a way to work out cubes by following set paths through the tables, using addition. From this, Babbage knew that a skillful engineer could design a system of cogwheels and rods that could be used to work out further cubes. Babbage began work on what he termed his difference engine in 1823. He built a demonstration model.

EXTENSION ACTIVITY

More

Logarithms / John Napier

Assess the importance of logarithms and John Napier's contribution to their calculation by reading these text.

1. Besides speeding up calculations, what were the consequences of the invention of logarithms? Formulate some hypotheses.
2. Could John Napier's activity as designer of war machines have influenced his work on logarithms? Why or why not? Justify your answer.

Weblink

The *Differential Engine* of Charles Babbage

Explore the functioning of the differential engine and the scientific theories that allowed it to be created.

1. Before the invention of the differential engine, what tools were most often used as calculating aids? Why were they often used for astronomy?
2. Compare and contrast the two accounts of the inspiration for Babbage's machine. In your opinion, which is more believable. Why?
3. How did the design of Babbage's machine evolve? How did it work? Explain it in your own words.

RUBRIC

Analyzing a Scientific Biography

Students will research the life of a scientific figure and present their findings. An exemplary biographical analysis will meet the following criteria.

- Illustrates strong knowledge of the subject
- Identifies the author of the biography
- Describes why the subject of the biography is important
- Contains information about the time and place in which the subject was born
- Lists important events in the subject's life
- Explains how events in the subject's life impacted him or her
- Makes inferences about the subject, based on events in his or her life
- Explains how the subject influenced the world while he or she lived
- Researches the cultural and historical context of the subject's life
- Examines the effect that the subject has had on the modern world
- Supplements information from the biography with independent research
- Organizes the analysis in a logical, effective manner
- Uses correct spelling, grammar, and punctuation
- Cites all sources used in the analysis

Ada Lovelace saw that it might be possible to apply the mechanical approach of Babbage's difference engine to qualities other than math, such as music.

Once the machine was started, it did not need further human intervention. In this sense, it can be described as the first automatic calculator. It was, however, very limited in scope. Inspired by Babbage's work, two Swedish engineers, Georg Scheutz and Edvard, his son, built a number of simplified difference engines. One was purchased by the Dudley Observatory in Albany, New York, and is now in the Smithsonian Institution in Washington, D.C.

In 1834, Babbage stopped work on the difference engine because of spiraling costs. He had put a great deal of his own money into the project but had also received grants from the government, which now decided that it had spent enough. By now, Babbage had begun to plan a more ambitious design for a general-purpose programmable computer that he called his analytical engine. In theory, the machine would be able to add, subtract, multiply, and divide any number of times in any order. It would also contain a memory store and a processing unit. The operating system, which was the equivalent of what today would be called the machine's software, would be provided by punched cards, a method that had been developed initially for use in the weaving industry. However, when Babbage approached the government for a financial grant to make this machine, it seems he was told that funds were not forthcoming.

First Computer Programmer

In the same year that work on the old engine stopped, Babbage met Ada Lovelace, who had come to hear him lecture. She was a well-connected young woman who had received a sound scientific education. She was the daughter of the scandalous poet Lord Byron and his wife, the wealthy heiress Annabella Milbanke. The marriage lasted only a year, but before they separated, Annabella gave birth to Ada. Soon afterward, Byron left England for good. Ada never saw her father again. A doctor told Annabella that her child should be taught science and mathematics to keep her "passions" under control. With the help of tutors, Ada learned geometry, **astronomy**, and mathematics.

Babbage's meeting with Lovelace had important consequences for them both. In 1842, the Italian engineer Luigi Menabrea published an account of the analytical engine. Babbage suggested that Lovelace translate it into English, and add her own observations. Lovelace showed how the analytical engine could be programmed with punched cards to generate an endless sequence of what mathematicians call Bernoulli numbers. For her development of this idea, Lovelace is often described as the first computer programmer.

Improvement and Change

By 1851, Babbage had given up hope of being able to construct the analytical engine. He kept revising his initial design of 1837, however, and his last plans for the analytical engine were produced as late as 1871. He left more than 6,000 pages of notes and some 300 engineering drawings of the machine. He told the mathematician John Moulton that he had not completed it because he was working on an idea for yet another calculating machine.

Babbage was a modernizer. If new industries were to be developed, he believed that new institutions, new technologies, and new attitudes to science were needed. He insisted that the institutions of British science were in need of reform. He repeated his concern that British mathematics was backward, and that the more powerful and simpler methods used in Europe were allowing French mathematics to flourish in contrast. Babbage also considered the role of science in society. He put forward proposals he thought would help modernize Britain, such as decimal currency, performance-related pay, and time-and-motion studies. It would be another 150 years before these ideas would be introduced.

Belated Recognition

By 1851, Ada Lovelace was deeply in debt. She was also addicted to laudanum, a liquid form of opium used as a painkiller. She died of cancer in 1852, aged 36.

Babbage died in London in 1871. Although he continued to work until his death on his analytical engine, it remained unbuilt. His contributions to computing were forgotten for many years, but he is now credited with having conceived the first automatic digital computer. The analytical engine has since been constructed from his original plans.

ADDING WITH COGWHEELS

Simple additions to create values below 10 can be made using a gear wheel with 10 cogs numbered from 0 to 9. An initial mark represents the starting point, or SP, which is aligned with 0. By moving the wheel three cogs clockwise, the cog numbered 3 is aligned with the SP. If the wheel is rotated a further 5 cogs, the SP will align with the number 8. Therefore, 5 and 3 added together make 8. However, if a further 5 is added, the number aligned with the SP will be 3, whereas 8 plus 5 equals 13.

The simplest solution to this problem had gear ratios of 10 cogs to one, where B has 10 cogs, while A has just one. When A makes a full revolution, B turns just one-tenth of a revolution, so 10 revolutions of wheel A will force just one complete turn of wheel B. To add 8 and 5, B is set at 0 and A at 8, and A is rotated five places. This moves the number 10 to the SP on B, and the number 3 to the SP on A, making a total of 13.

To make additions creating values running into the hundreds, further geared wheels can be added to the shaft of B. Theoretically, the process can carry on for ever, though adding extra shafts and gears increases the risk of mechanical failure.

These gear wheels have a ratio of 10 cogs to one.

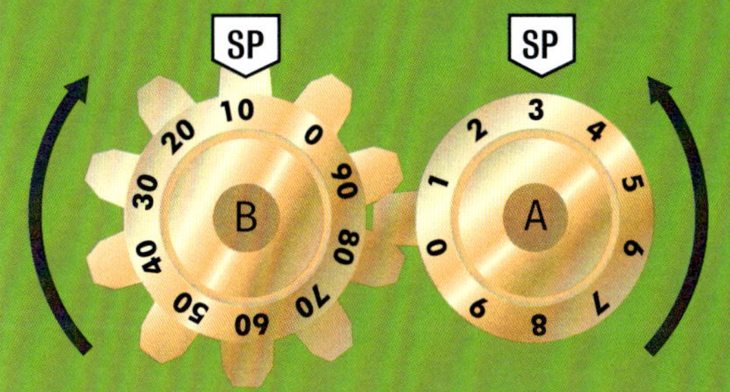

EXTENSION ACTIVITY

Document

The diplomas of Charles Babbage

Examine the diplomas and certificates obtained by Charles Babbage during his lifetime.

1. Who gave these diplomas to Babbage? Why was he given them? Postulate about the possible reasons.
2. From where did he receive these diplomas? Why are they carefully preserved? What do they tell us about the importance of Babbage's scientific work?

Weblink

Ada Lovelace: Victorian computing visionary

Explore Ada Lovelace's life and achievements in the field of computer science.

1. How did Ada Lovelace's family history influence her intellectual development and scientific achievements? Would these have been the same, had she lived and grown in a different family context? Why or why not? Justify your answer.
2. In what ways did Ada Lovelace's approach to Babbage's calculus aid engine differ? How did she contribute to the development and improvement of Babbage's work?

THOMAS ALVA EDISON

1847–1931

Perhaps the greatest inventor of all time, Thomas A. Edison took out more than 1,000 patents. His inventions helped create the modern way of life. They included the electric light bulb, the movie projector, the electric typewriter, and the early gramophone.

Thomas Edison's father ran a successful lumber business in Milan, Ohio, until the family moved to Port Huron, Michigan. Edison began school when he was eight years old, but after only three months, his mother taught him at home. Thereafter, Edison was mainly self taught, learning from books and from ceaseless experimentation.

These characteristics were evident when he took his first job at age 12 as a newsboy on the Detroit to Port Huron railroad. To supplement his earnings, he sold fruit and candy to passengers and soon had other boys working for him. One day, he noticed an empty freight car on the train. Edison had earned enough to buy a hand printing press, which he set up in the car. He wrote, printed, and sold 400 copies of a news sheet, the *Grand Trunk Herald*. In 1863, Edison began work in the Port Huron telegraph office as an apprentice. In its day, the electric telegraph had an enormous impact on society.

The Telegraph Network

The first telegraph line, which opened in 1844, linked Washington and Baltimore. The new industry attracted a group of young men who were fascinated by the new technology. For five years after 1863, Edison was part of this traveling community, working in many parts of the country. As an expert telegrapher, he always found it easy to get a job. In 1868, however, Edison's hearing began to fail. No one knows the cause. He never went completely deaf, but holding quiet conversations became difficult. As a consequence of his deafness, he had to give up working as a telegrapher.

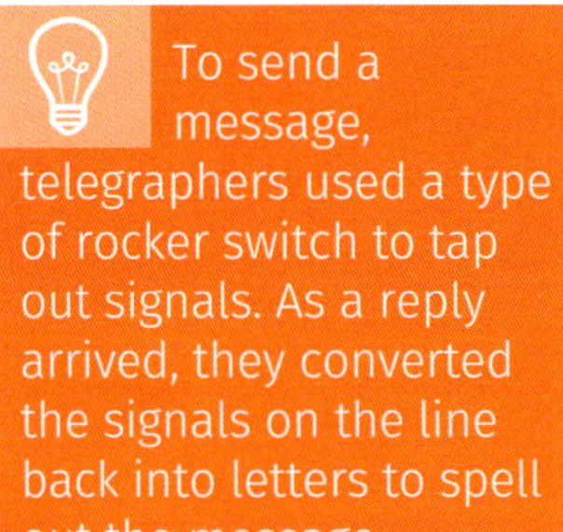

To send a message, telegraphers used a type of rocker switch to tap out signals. As a reply arrived, they converted the signals on the line back into letters to spell out the message.

Freelance Inventor

In 1869, Edison decided to become a freelance inventor. His first inventions were connected with telegraphy. Edison's universal stock printer was a "stock ticker," a machine that printed out changing prices on the Stock Exchange. Western Union bought the machine from him. He then went on to develop the duplex. This device doubled the capacity of a telegraph wire by allowing operators to send messages in both directions at the same time. In 1874, Edison invented the quadruplex, which allowed the transmission of two messages each way. Railroad baron Jay Gould paid Edison more than $100,000 for the rights to this invention, despite Western Union's prior claims to it. This was to involve Edison in years of litigation.

Effective Light Bulbs

In 1876, Edison established his own laboratory and machine shop in Menlo Park, New Jersey. With two associates, Charles Batchelor, a master mechanic and draftsman, and John Kruesi, a Swiss-born machinist, he began working on a wide range of experiments. One of the men's first areas of investigation was electric lighting.

45 words The number of words per minute **Edison could send as a telegraph operator**

In 1904, Edison employed **450** people at his factory **making accumulator batteries for electric cars.**

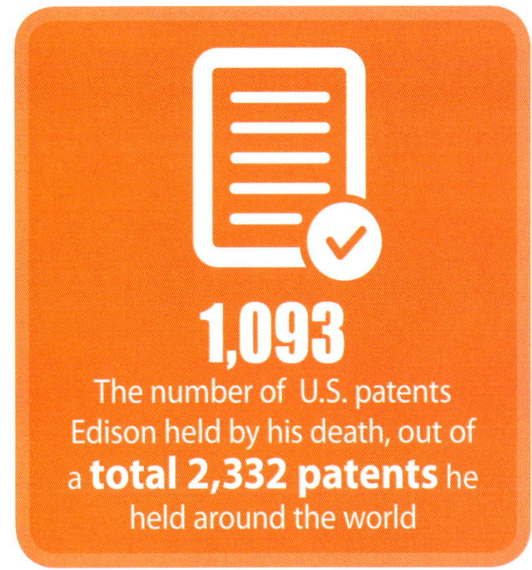

1,093 The number of U.S. patents Edison held by his death, out of a **total 2,332 patents** he held around the world

EXTENSION ACTIVITY

More

Morse Code

Analyze the importance of Morse Code and how it works.

1. Why is the inventor of Morse code, Samuel Morse, described as "the true founder of the electric telegraph industry"? Justify your answer.
2. Why was Morse Code used for telegraphing? What other codes could have been used with a telegraph? Formulate some hypotheses.

Document

Edison's patents

Explore the collection of Edison's 1,093 patents.

1. What is the purpose of a patent? Why did Edison register so many patents? Formulate some theories.
2. Select one patent. What information does the patent report? Why does the patent report that specific information? How is the patented invention described in the patent?
3. Compare and contrast your findings with another of Edison's patents. How are they similar? How do they differ?

Edison made many observations as he experimented to create a vacuum-filled light bulb that would produce a bright light without the filament burning out.

In 1808, English scientist Humphry Davy had connected wires from an electrical battery to two carbon rods and produced a white glow. Davy's device was the first arc lamp. Although arc lighting replaced gas lighting in some areas, it had limited uses. The light was very bright and hot, and the lamps smelled bad.

A better option was the incandescent lamp, in which light is produced by heating a thin wire. When an **electric current** is passed through a filament, it heats up and emits light. The filament completely burned away when mixed with oxygen in the air, however. The answer was to enclose the filament in a glass globe from which the air had been pumped out. In the absence of an efficient vacuum pump, this was not an easy task. Nor was it obvious which material would make the best filament.

The first choice was carbon, the element with the highest melting point. In 1877, Edison tested charred, or carbonized paper, but found that it burned up too quickly. Edison then tried the metal platinum, but it failed to produce a satisfactory light and was extremely expensive. Edison often worked days and nights at a stretch and expected his assistants to do the same. Sometimes he took brief naps on a lab bench before carrying on. In all, he tested more than 1,600 materials. "I have not failed," he remarked of the tests. "I have just found 10,000 ways that won't work."

A Breakthrough at Last

The first real progress came when Edison heard that a new vacuum pump was available. It had been invented in 1852 by the German chemist Herman Sprengel. The new Sprengel pump allowed Edison to consider carbon filaments again. In October 1879, Edison noted that a carbon filament had worked for 13.5 hours. A few days later, he recorded a filament that had burned for 170 hours. On November 1, he applied for a patent for a carbon-filament lamp and began to produce his new bulb in quantity. He later found that carbonized bamboo performed better as a filament.

In 1882, Edison produced 100,000 bulbs in a single year. Within 20 years, he was selling 45 million a year. The light bulb itself was later considerably improved. The invention of a glass-blowing machine in 1903 meant that large quantities of light bulbs could be produced quickly, and an inert gas such as argon was used in the bulb to lengthen the life of the filament. In 1911, the carbon filament was replaced by tungsten. Tungsten can be drawn into thin wires. A 7-inch (18-cm) length no thicker than a pencil lead can make 100 miles (160 km) of filament. Tungsten also produces a white light rather than the yellow light of the carbon filament.

Power for All

In 1882, Edison opened an **electricity** generating station in New York City. By the end of the following year, he had acquired 431 customers and was supplying power to more than 2,000 lamps. At the same time, Edison and his English partner, the physicist Joseph Swan, opened a power station in London, England. The age of electricity had arrived. At first, the new power seemed very strange to customers used to gas, and electricity did not become common in homes for some years. By 1914, about 10 percent of U.S. homes had electricity, and in other countries, the figure was lower. In the nineteenth century, it was still mainly used for public lighting, gradually replacing gas lamps in streets, factories, theaters, and stores. Later, it was used to power transportation. In 1903, the first electric tram service came into service in London.

Electricity was also adopted as a method of executing convicted criminals. Edison did not want the public to think of him when they thought of the electric chair, so he proposed that the electricity system of his rival, George Westinghouse, should be used instead.

SWITCHING CIRCUITS

In 1878, Edison established the Electric Light Company to find a safe, cheap alternative to gas lighting. To do this, he had to find a suitable electrical circuit. In a series circuit, all the lights on the system are joined in succession in a continuous circuit. That meant they would either be on or off at the same time. Edison proposed to connect his lights in a parallel circuit by subdividing the current to run through different wires. This could be done only by using a high-resistance system. Resistance is the opposition to the flow of current presented by the various parts of a circuit, which is measured in ohms. Current traveling through a low-resistance system generates heat and requires thick, expensive copper cable. By contrast, a high-resistance system restricts the volume of the current. It is more efficient because less current generates less heat. At the time, however, no high-resistance light bulb had yet been invented. This inspired Edison to begin his search.

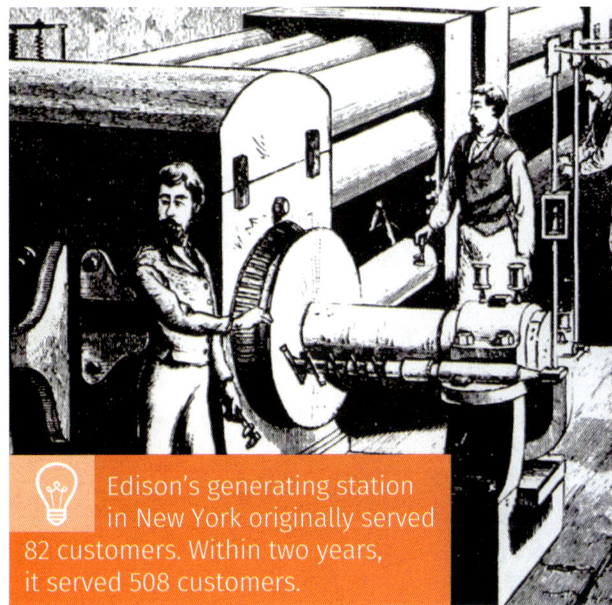

Edison's generating station in New York originally served 82 customers. Within two years, it served 508 customers.

EXTENSION ACTIVITY

More

Joseph Swan

Review the text about the life of Joseph Swan.

1. What was the contribution of Joseph Swan to Edison's inventions? Formulate some hypotheses.
2. In your opinion, why did Swan and Edison decide to merge their companies? Discuss some possible reasons.

Weblink

Edison's Pearl Street Station Recognized With Milestone

Analyze the photo gallery and article reporting the recognition of Pearl Street Station as a "Milestone in Electrical Engineering and Computing."

1. Why was this title awarded to Pearl Street Station? Do you agree with the awarding of this title? Why or why not?
2. What information did the 2008 archaeological excavation give us about Pearl Street Station? In your opinion, what is the significance of the remains of an 1890s facility? What possible reasons might there have been for the archaeological excavation?

The Phonograph

Edison began developing the phonograph, a machine for recording sound, as early as 1877. Earlier inventors had suggested that sounds, if they could be graphically recorded, would produce distinct shapes. Edison set out to try to do this. He used a carbon transmitter with a stylus tip to make indentations in a strip of paraffined paper. When the paper was pulled back beneath the stylus, a vague series of sounds was generated. He had managed to record sound as graphical marks and play it back. His next model used a sheet of grooved tinfoil wrapped around a horizontal cylinder.

Edison demonstrated his phonograph in December 1877. It had three main parts, which were a cone-shaped speaking tube, a hand-cranked cylinder covered with tinfoil, and a playback device. Speaking into the tube caused a thin sheet called a diaphragm to vibrate. A needle connected to the diaphragm left a pattern of grooves on the rotating foil. When Edison rewound the cylinder and played it back, his voice was heard emerging faintly from the tube.

Improvements followed. An electric motor was added, a funnel amplified the sound, and wax replaced the tinfoil. Although Edison thought the machine would be used by business people to dictate letters, the public mainly used the new machine to play recorded music. The phonograph was soon overtaken in popularity by the disk gramophone, which was invented in 1888 by German-born Emile Berliner.

Edison's first recording with his phonograph, or "sound writer," was his own voice reciting the nursery rhyme "Mary Had a Little Lamb."

The Lights Go Out

By 1886, Edison had set up a laboratory in West Orange, New Jersey, as a scientific research facility. There, he continued to develop the phonograph and laid the foundations of the motion picture industry. He invented an alkaline storage battery that was used in submarines and designed a battery for use on Ford's Model T car. During the late 1880s and early 1890s, he became involved in a disastrous magnetic ore-mining venture, which he financed using most of his General Electric Company shares. He spent the years of World War I (1914–1918) chairing a scientific advisory committee and finding ways of detecting torpedoes.

Edison carried on working well into his eighties. Since the 1870s, he had been one of the best-known people in the world. On the announcement of his death in 1931, all lights in the United States were extinguished for one minute in his honor.

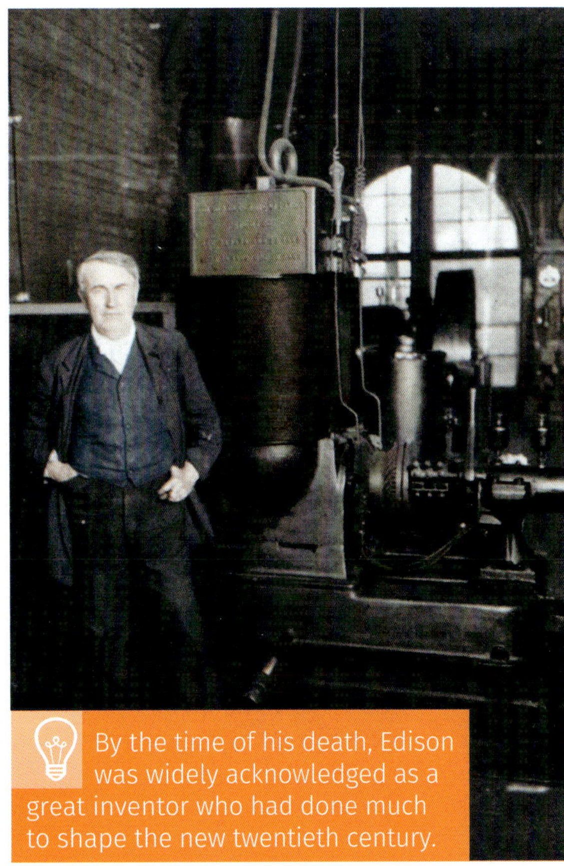

By the time of his death, Edison was widely acknowledged as a great inventor who had done much to shape the new twentieth century.

GEORGE WESTINGHOUSE

George Westinghouse was a U.S. engineer and inventor. He learned his trade making and maintaining agricultural machinery, and then he served in the Union Army during the Civil War (1861–1865) and later as an engineer in the U.S. Navy. In 1865, Westinghouse invented a device for getting derailed railroad cars back onto the rails. Three years later, he produced a cast-steel "frog" for railroad switches. The frog is the V-shaped piece that fits where the rails fork. In 1872, Westinghouse perfected his most famous invention, a brake for railroad vehicles that used compressed air generated by the locomotive. Within 20 years, air brakes were compulsory on all trains in the United States.

In 1886, Westinghouse founded the Westinghouse Electric Company. He championed the use of high-voltage alternating current, or AC, for the distribution of electric power. This brought him into conflict with Edison, who introduced a direct-current, or DC, distribution. Eventually, Westinghouse's alternating current received nationwide acceptance.

EXTENSION ACTIVITY

More

Moving Pictures

Analyze the first experiments with moving photography.

1. In your opinion, why did photography stimulate curiosity for moving images and many experiments at the end of the 19th century? Formulate some hypotheses.
2. Why did Edison buy the right for the Vitascope to compete with the Lumière brothers instead of merging with their company as he did with Joseph Swan's? Discuss some possible reasons.

Weblink

History of the Cylinder Phonograph

Explore the evolution and history of the cylinder phonograph invented by Thomas Edison.

1. Compare and contrast the different possible uses of the phonograph listed by Edison. How many of these are still current uses of sound registration and reproduction devices? How do our uses of these devices compare with the ones proposed by Edison for his phonograph? How are they similar? How are they different?
2. How was Edison's invention received by the public? How did this reception evolve with the different models of the phonograph?

RUBRIC

Analyzing a Primary Source

Students will complete a thorough analysis of a primary source. An exemplary analysis will meet the following criteria.

- Identifies the creator of the source
- Explains what medium was used to create the primary source
- Describes why the source qualifies as a primary one
- Explores any literary devices used in the source
- Identifies the intended audience for the source
- Relates the creator's goals in creating the source
- Illustrates knowledge of the period and location in which the source was created
- Distinguishes between facts and opinions found in the source
- Examines the reliability of the source's creator
- Compares the source with similar documents
- Cites additional sources used in the analysis
- Presents information in a clear, concise manner
- Uses correct spelling, grammar, and punctuation

ALEXANDER GRAHAM BELL

1847–1922

Alexander Graham Bell is best known for inventing the telephone. The device transformed communications worldwide. Bell also developed many other ideas, such as the electric telegraph, hydrofoils, and aircraft.

Alexander Graham Bell was born in Edinburgh, Scotland, in 1847. His education was largely gained at home. After spending a year in London in 1862, Alexander returned to Scotland, where he taught music and elocution. In 1868, Bell moved back to London and began work as assistant to his father, Melville. In 1870, Alexander's older brother, also named Melville, died of tuberculosis at the age of 25. His younger brother had died of the same disease two years earlier. Alexander and his parents emigrated to Canada, which was thought to be a healthy place to live.

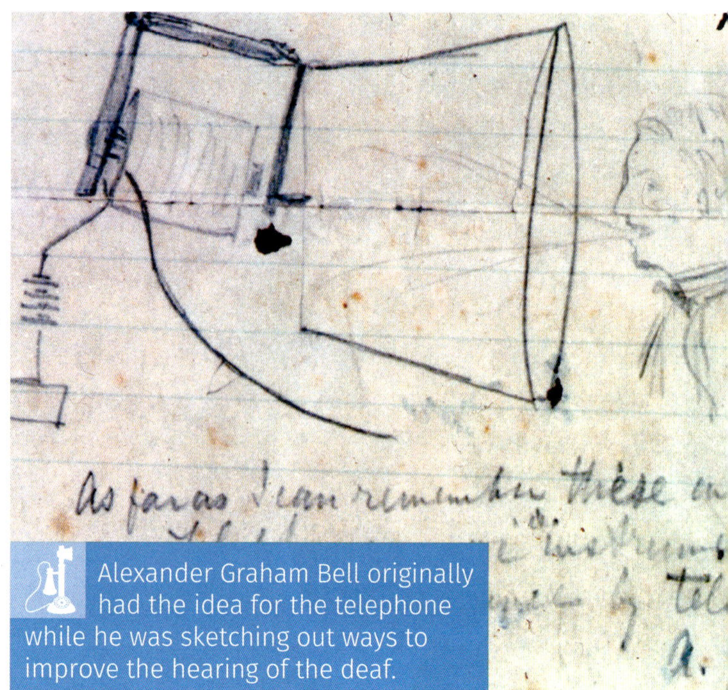

Alexander Graham Bell originally had the idea for the telephone while he was sketching out ways to improve the hearing of the deaf.

In Canada, Bell's father began to lecture on a way of writing down speech he had invented, called "Visible Speech." The system used diagrams to show the positions of the tongue, teeth, and lips. It was intended to be used to teach the hard of hearing to speak. The Boston School for the Deaf was interested in adopting the system, and in 1871, invited Melville Bell to show them how it worked. Alexander went instead and quickly established a practice in Boston working with the hard of hearing. By 1873, he had become professor of vocal physiology at Boston University.

Help for the Hard of Hearing

Much of Bell's early work concerned devices to help the hard of hearing to communicate. He first tried to make a "phonautograph," which aimed to convert speech into written patterns. In this way, the hard of hearing could check their own speech.

In the course of developing his machine, Bell experimented with various types of membranes in order to try to imitate the way the human eardrum worked. The eardrum is a thin, semitransparent, pliable structure. Bell wondered how it could move the solid bones of the inner ear. If a thin membrane could do such heavy work, it might also respond to sound waves by modifying the flow of an electric current.

Initial experiments were unsuccessful, however. Bell was able to take his work further only because Gardiner Greene Hubbard, a wealthy Boston attorney, offered to finance him. Hubbard's daughter, Mabel, had become deaf at the age of five after contracting scarlet fever. She was a pupil of Bell's, and Hubbard was impressed by Bell's efforts on her behalf. In 1877, Mabel and Bell were married.

Bell spent his early career helping teach the hard of hearing to feel the vibrations in their throats as they spoke. This helped them to communicate better.

Sending Words with Electricity

Bell did not set out to invent the telephone. He originally tried to develop a "harmonic" or "multiple telegraph," a device that could receive several telegraph messages at once. In 1874, he took on a young mechanic named Thomas Watson as an assistant. Together, they worked on trying to develop another idea of Bell's. This was a device that would be able to transmit speech using electricity.

The principles behind Bell's work derive from the research of Danish physicist Hans Christian Oersted and English chemist and physicist Michael Faraday. In 1820, Oersted discovered that, if he passed an electric current through a wire, it generated a magnetic field around it. In 1831, Faraday proved that disturbances in this magnetic field can generate an electric current, the strength of which depends on how much the magnetic field is disturbed. This is known as "induction." It produces an "induced" current.

EXTENSION ACTIVITY

More

Thomas Augustus Watson

Review the text about the life of Thomas Augustus Watson

1. In your opinion, what was unique about Watson's professional path later in life? Would a similar career path be more common today? Why or why not?
2. Could Thomas Augustus Watson be described as an inventor? What was his role in the development of the telephone?

First Hand

Letter from Alexander Graham Bell to Henry S. Redfield

Analyze the letter written by Alexander Graham Bell dated July 23, 1897.

1. What does Alexander Graham Bell recommend for the benefit of the hearing impaired children? Why? Justify your answer.
2. Why did Alexander Graham Bell think hearing impaired children should be "under the same educational influences as [. . .] hearing children"? How does this approach compare to current approaches in the education of young hearing impaired students? How is it different or similar?

RUBRIC

Create a Scientific Drawing

Create a scientific drawing illustrating an object or design. An exemplary scientific drawing will meet the following criteria.

- Includes a descriptive and accurate title
- The drawing(s) realistically depicts the object(s)
- The drawing only includes features that were actually observed
- Relevant details such as size, colors, textures, shapes, and relationships to surroundings are included
- Multiple perspectives are drawn to provide the viewer with a complete picture
- All parts of the scientific drawing are clearly labeled with the correct terms
- A written explanation of the drawing shows what is included in the drawing
- A key or legend is provided
- An appropriate size and scale is chosen for the drawing so that the details are easily recognized

Bell hired Thomas Watson as his assistant in 1874. Watson later went on to have a short career as an actor before becoming an important shipbuilder.

Making a Breakthrough

A tuning fork consists of two metal prongs that vibrate to produce a note. Bell linked a tuning fork to an electromagnet. The strength of the current induced by the electromagnet depended on the pitch of the vibrating prongs. This current could flow through a wire to a second electromagnet and produce the same note in a second tuning fork. Bell hoped forks tuned to different frequencies might be used to send different messages at the same time.

The breakthrough came in June 1875. Vibrating reeds had taken the place of tuning forks in Bell's device. One of the reeds stopped vibrating, and Watson gave it a tap. In a distant room, Bell heard a loud twang, meaning the sound had been transmitted. On February 14, 1876, Bell filed a telephone patent application, giving him the right to be the only person to make and sell his invention. A few hours later, another patent for a telephone was filed from a rival, Elisha Gray. This would lead to the first of many challenges to Bell's patent. On March 7, the Patent Office issued the patent to Bell for "the method of, and apparatus for, transmitting vocal or other sound telegraphically ... by causing electrical undulations..."

Bell's notebook entry of March 10, 1876, describes the exciting events of the day. Watson took his place in one room with the "Receiving Instrument," and Bell took up position in another room next to the "Transmitting Instrument." Bell shouted into the transmitter, "Mr. Watson—Come here—I want to see you," and his notebook records what happened next. "To my delight he came and declared that he had heard and understood what I said. We then changed places.... The sentence, 'Mr. Bell, do you understand what I say? Do—you—un—der—stand—what—I—say?' came quite clearly." The new invention stole the show at the 1876 Centennial Exhibition in Philadelphia.

New Projects

Bell continued to work on methods of communication. His next project was the "photophone," or light-sounder. In the 1870s, it was discovered that the electrical resistance of the element selenium varied with the intensity of the light falling on it. Bell thought this might be a way to transmit speech. A speaker's voice made a beam of light vibrate. The vibrating light beam was directed onto a piece of selenium, altering its resistance and creating a varying electric current that was turned back into sound. Although Bell achieved some success with the device, investors were more interested in putting money into the new telephone system.

Alexander Graham Bell was skilled at promoting his inventions. He made many public demonstrations of devices, such as the telephone.

Bell's curiosity had already led him onto a range of other projects. In 1901, he invented the tetrahedral kite, a kite with four triangular sides. Bell built large versions, capable of carrying people. He also tried to develop a reliable hydrofoil. A hydrofoil is a boat that has "wings" under the hull that raise the hull out of the water. This reduces drag and allows the boat to travel faster than a normal craft. Another quest was Bell's attempt to develop a "vacuum jacket." His baby son, Edward, had died in 1881 of breathing problems. Bell set out to design a jacket that would help people breathe by reducing air pressure around the body so that atmospheric pressure forced air through the mouth and into the lungs. This type of device would become the "iron lung," which was widely used to help patients with the disease polio.

Bell died on August 2, 1922. As he told a reporter a few months earlier, he had continued trying to "seek answers for his unceasing hows and whys about things."

BELL LABORATORIES

After his death, Bell's name was given to one of the world's most important scientific institutions, the Bell Laboratories. Known as the Bell Lab, it was founded in 1925 with a staff of 3,000 and located in Murray Hill, New Jersey. By 1983, the Bell Lab had been granted 20,000 patents, and its staff had won seven **Nobel prizes**. It was particularly known for the invention of the transistor, a **semiconductor** with three connections, which allows the modification of electrical flow in electronic devices. The transistor was developed in 1947 by William Shockley, Walter Brattain, and John Bardeen. They received the 1956 Nobel Prize for Physics for their work.

EXTENSION ACTIVITY

More

Legal Challenges

Examine the legal challenges Bell had to face in defending his rights to the telephone patent.

1. Why was it necessary to register a patent? What were the advantages? Were there any possible disadvantages to owning a patent?
2. In your opinion, why did Western Union refuse to buy Bell's patent in 1876, then challenge him in court at a later date? Formulate some hypotheses.

Document

Drawing by Alexander Graham Bell

Examine the 1876 drawing by Alexander Graham Bell.

1. What does the drawing represent? What was its purpose? What insights does it give us into Bell's research?
2. Decipher the text at the bottom of the page. How is the telephone described? Without the benefit of the text, what other inventions could the drawing be depicting?

RUBRIC

Analyzing a Scientific Video

Students will watch and assess a video related to a scientific discovery, and write an analysis of the video. An exemplary video analysis will meet the following criteria.

- Identifies the purpose of the video
- Identifies the intended audience of the video
- Identifies the video as a primary or secondary source
- Discusses the scientific and social context of the video
- Describes how the content of the video is presented
- Summarizes the information and opinions presented in the video
- Analyzes the quality of the content presented in the video
- Assesses the effectiveness of the video
- Determines whether the images and graphics used in the video relate to the content
- Determines whether the video is easy to follow and understand
- Gives the analysis a clear and consistent purpose
- Organizes the analysis in a logical, effective manner
- Presents a strong, clear argument about the video
- Provides strong and accurate details to support the argument about the video
- Considers other perspectives on the purpose and effectiveness of the video
- Cites all sources used in the analysis

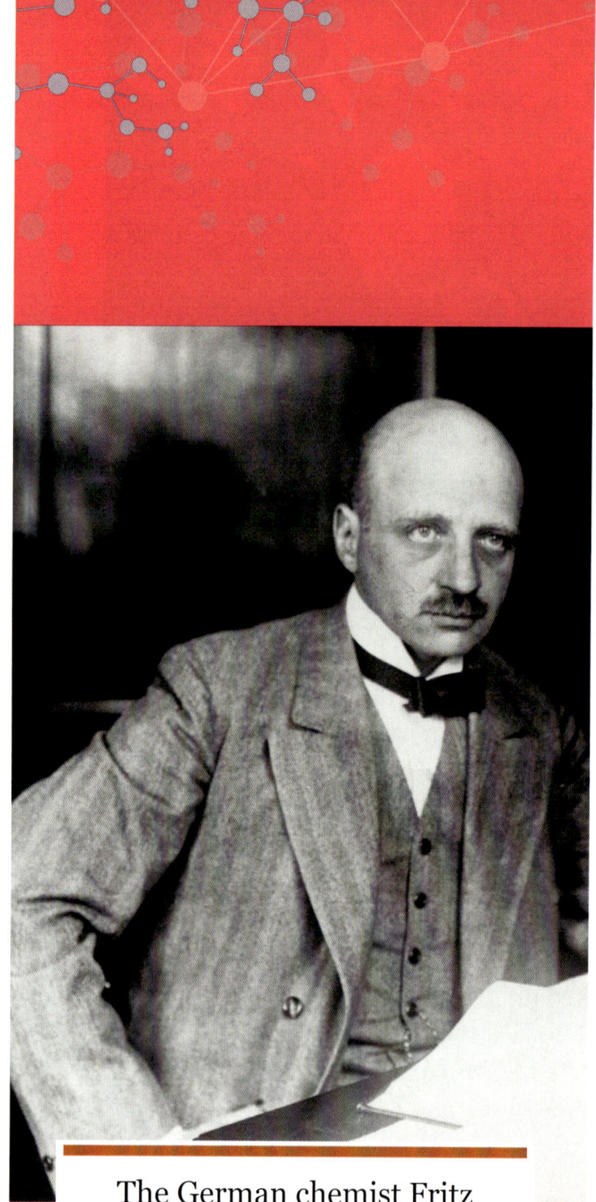

The German chemist Fritz Haber gave his name to the Haber process. This was a method of creating the gas ammonia. Ammonia was used in fertilizers as well as in explosives, which were both substances Germany needed during World War I.

FRITZ HABER
1868–1934

Fritz Haber was born in Breslau, Silesia, in 1868, to a German-Jewish family. Silesia was then part of Prussia. Three years later, Prussia became part of the newly formed German empire, or Second Reich. Haber's father was a trader in natural dyes, and after studying at the German universities of Berlin and Heidelberg, and at Zürich in Switzerland, Haber joined the family business as a salesman. He quit after a disagreement with his father over the future of synthetic dyes, which are dyes produced artificially through a chemical reaction.

Haber secured a post in the Department of Chemical and Fuel Technology at the Karlsruhe Technical University in Germany. His work at Karlsruhe would have two dramatically different effects. On one hand, it would save the world from hunger. On the other, it would create a way of killing and disabling many thousands of people quickly and efficiently.

Need for Nitrates

In 1840, German chemist Justus von Liebig concluded that among the "foods" needed by plants were **nitrogen** and potassium. He thought plants got nitrogen from the air. In fact, they absorb nutrients from the soil. When land is farmed year after year, plant yields get lower unless nutrients are returned to the soil via fertilizers. Traditional farming used animal manure as a fertilizer, but the world's population was rapidly growing at the end of the nineteenth century, so more food was needed. More and more land was coming into production, so huge amounts of fertilizer were needed. It was not clear, however, where it could be found.

For a time, Chile saltpeter, or sodium nitrate, provided the answer. Deposits of the natural chemical were running out, however. At the start of the twentieth century, scientists warned that a chemical solution must be found to the problem.

The issue was particularly serious in Germany. In the years leading up to World War I (1914–1918), Germany was concentrating its resources on becoming a leading world power. Nitrates, or salts containing nitrogen, were not only essential for fertilizers. They were also vital in many explosives. Leaders in Germany realized that, if there was a major war, German ports would be cut off from supplies of nitrates. Nitrates could be recovered from ammonia, a compound of nitrogen and hydrogen, but ammonia was expensive to make. What was needed was a way of making ammonia by synthesizing it from nitrogen in the atmosphere and hydrogen extracted from coal gas. Earlier attempts to make nitrogen react with hydrogen by using electric sparks had failed because a temperature of 5,432° Fahrenheit (3,000° Celsius) was required.

When chemists cannot get a desired chemical reaction, they often try catalysts.A catalyst is a substance that speeds up a chemical reaction. Haber therefore tried to combine nitrogen and hydrogen using a suitable catalyst. Eventually, in 1903, he succeeded in combining nitrogen and hydrogen at a temperature of 1,832°F (1,000°C) using iron as a catalyst. The yields, however, were too small to be commercially useful. A colleague, Walther Nernst, pointed out that increasing the pressure might help the reaction, and Haber figured out how much extra pressure would be needed to create a productive reaction.

Fritz Haber quit the family dye business when his father refused to trade in popular new synthetic dyes, which created a wide range of more vivid colors.

By 1909, Haber had established that he could produce large quantities of ammonia with an iron catalyst at a temperature of 932°F (500°C) and a relatively high pressure. Commercial production of ammonia by the Haber process began in 1913, the year before World War I began. By 1918, thanks to Haber, Germany remained virtually self-sufficient in its supply of this vital chemical throughout the years of fighting.

An Untimely Award

In 1911, Haber became director of the Kaiser Wilhelm Institute for Physical **Chemistry** in Berlin. On the outbreak of war in August 1914, he put his laboratory at the disposal of the German government. He became a key figure in the development of poison gas as a weapon.

EXTENSION ACTIVITY

More

Synthetic Dyes
Examine the evolution of synthetic dyes.

1. Why did Fritz Haber think that trade in natural dyes was "doomed"? Were his feelings founded or unfounded? Defend your position with evidence.
2. In your opinion, why was the discovery of a formula for a synthetic indigo dye awarded the Nobel prize? Justify your answer.

Video

The source of nitrates—The chemistry of almost everything
Review Fritz Haber's most important discoveries by watching the video.

1. What were the main sources of nitrates before Haber's discovery? In your opinion, what was the main reason behind Fritz Haber's research on production of nitrates? Develop arguments to support your response.
2. Why was this research carried out during this historical period? Formulate some theories.
3. What other discoveries have led to starkly different consequences? How were they beneficial? In what ways were they harmful?

EXTENSION ACTIVITY

Analyzing Speeches as Arguments

Students will analyze a speech as an argument and write a response. An exemplary analysis will meet the following criteria.

- Presents a strong thesis that is based on analysis of the argument presented in the speech and how the argument is presented
- Consistently uses strong textual evidence to support the thesis
- Presents an engaging and effective introduction, body, and conclusion
- Structures the analysis in a logical order
- Develops a thorough analysis of the speech
- Identifies the main points presented in the speech
- Identifies the speaker and infers how his or her life may have shaped this argument
- Identifies when and where the speech was given
- Determines the speech's intended audience
- Uses strong evidence from the speech to show how the speaker supports his or her argument
- Analyzes the language used to convey the speech's argument
- Demonstrates understanding of the historical and societal context in which the speech was given and connects that context to the speech's argument
- Properly integrates quotations
- Properly cites all sources used

In 1918, Haber was awarded the Nobel Prize for Chemistry "for the synthesis of ammonia from its elements, nitrogen and hydrogen." The process that Haber invented had produced weapons responsible for the death and disablement of millions of people in the war, so it seemed to many people that this was an odd award to make at this time. Many French and British scientists felt that Haber's role in developing German chemical warfare made him unfit to receive such an award. They expressed their belief that he had "initiated a mode of warfare which is to the everlasting discredit of Germany."

Gold from the Sea

Ever the patriot, Haber sought another way to serve his country. At the end of World War I, the Allies ordered Germany to pay a very large fine as a punishment. Some of this was to be paid in gold. The Allies hoped such costs would halt any military aggression by Germany. Haber knew that the world's oceans contained billions of tons (metric tons) of gold, and he began to try to recover this gold from seawater and so help free Germany from its huge debts. In 1923, he set up a laboratory on the liner *Hansa* and began trying to extract gold from the Atlantic Ocean. The project was unsuccessful and was abandoned in 1927.

Victim of the Nazis

After the war, Haber's institute in Berlin became the world's leading center of research in physical chemistry. Haber had close links with industry, and he began building relations with foreign scientists. In 1930, he founded the Japan Institute, which had bases in Berlin and Tokyo, Japan, to forge closer scientific links between the two countries.

In January 1933, Adolf Hitler became chancellor of Germany. The Nazi Party he led blamed Jews for the country's economic and social problems, and it passed a series of harsh anti-Jewish laws. In April 1933, a new Civil Service Law prevented the employment of anyone not of pure German descent.

German forces used poison gas at Ypres in Belgium in April 1915. The British and French also soon began using gas as a weapon.

Gas attacks left soldiers unable to breathe properly, and many victims died. A large number of survivors were blinded.

All university teachers and professors in Germany were employed by the state. Very large numbers of them, particularly scientists and doctors, were Jewish. Hitler stated that, if the loss of Jewish scientists meant the "annihilation of German science, then we shall do without science for a few years." For Jewish scientists, however distinguished or old, leaving Germany was the only sensible course of action. The costs of leaving the country were high. It meant abandoning the family home, all financial assets, and perhaps a laboratory or a professional position built up over a lifetime. Non-Jewish German scientists looked on hopelessly as they saw the might of German science dwindle away before their eyes. Nobel prize-winners, mathematicians, physicists, and chemists were all forced to flee their own country.

Haber was Jewish. At first, his leading position, famous patriotism, and previous service to the state gave him some protection. Veterans of the 1914–1918 war were exempt from the Civil Service Law. Unofficially, Haber was told that his position was secure, as long as he made no fuss. Haber did not accept this, however, and resigned his post. There was no turning back. He left Germany for the final time in the summer of 1933.

He had been invited to work in Cambridge, England, by Sir William Pope, the chemist who had led Great Britain's own chemical warfare program. Haber worked in Cambridge for only a brief period. Soon after his move to England, while on vacation in Switzerland on January 29, 1934, he died of a heart attack.

HABER PROCESS

During the Haber process, nitrogen from liquefied air reacts with hydrogen from coal gas at high temperatures and pressure to produce ammonia, which is condensed to produce liquid ammonia.

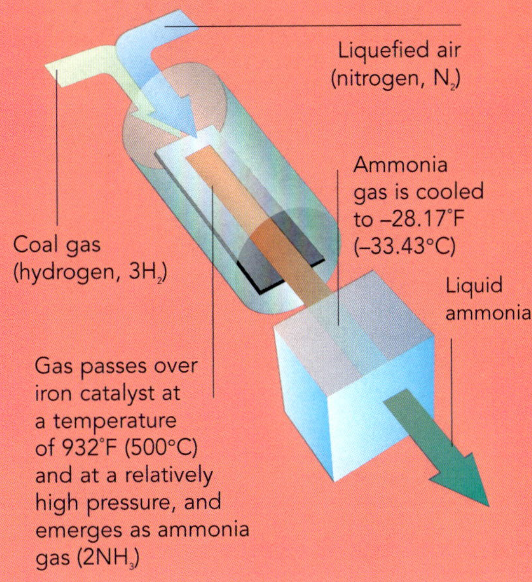

EXTENSION ACTIVITY

More

Chemical Warfare

Explore the use of gases in warfare.

1. Why were chemical weapons banned by the Hague convention? How did the Germans and Allied forces justify the use of such weapons despite the convention? Would that be possible today? Support your answers with examples.
2. In your opinion, why did Haber support the use of these weapons? Do you agree or disagree with Haber? Defend your position.

Document

Award Ceremony Speech

Analyze the speech given by Å.G. Ekstrand, President of the Royal Swedish Academy of Sciences, when Fritz Haber was presented with the Nobel Prize for Chemistry.

1. In what terms did Ekstrand describe Haber's achievements? Did he refer to the World War? How did he speak of Haber's involvement in the War? Why? Justify your answer using excerpts from the text.
2. What other methods were developed for the production of nitrates before Haber's discovery? Why were they not used? How did Haber's system differ from other methods? Cite examples to explain your response.

ALAN TURING
1912–1954

Alan Turing led the way for the development of computers. He imagined the potential of artificial intelligence, or the ability of a computer to perform tasks as a human might. He was also instrumental in cracking the secret codes used by the Germans in World War II (1939–1945).

Alan Mathison Turing was born in London on June 23, 1912. At age 13, his parents sent him to Sherborne, a boarding school in southwest England, but he was not particularly happy there. However, Turing was outstandingly talented at mathematics. At school, he sought refuge from loneliness in the science laboratory, where he often carried out chemistry experiments in his own time. Turing then befriended another boy called Christopher Morcom, who shared his love of mathematics and science. Early in 1931, however, Morcom became sick and died suddenly. Turing was devastated.

Turing theorized that it should be possible to give a machine a set of instructions that would enable it to play games based on logical rules, such as chess.

The most important part of Turing's career coincided with World War II. Turing would lead the British effort to decode signals sent from German U-boats, or submarines.

In October 1931, Turing went to study mathematics at King's College, which is part of Cambridge University. He completed his studies in 1934. Thanks to his outstanding talent for mathematics, after his graduation, he stayed at Kings and took up a graduate research position.

Search for Mathematical Logic

Early in 1935, Turing attended some lectures by Max Newman, a British mathematician with an interest in mathematical logic. This is the branch of science concerned with the role of mathematics in formal analysis. At the beginning of the twentieth century, mathematicians were very interested in the question of whether all mathematical truths could be derived from purely logical foundations. A key figure in the field was the British philosopher Bertrand Russell. Together with the English mathematician Alfred North Whitehead, Russell wrote *Principia Mathematica* (1910–1913). Whitehead and Russell believed that their book contained a complete, logical system within which all valid mathematical formulas could be proved.

Max Newman's lectures covered this work, as well as that of the Austrian-born American philosopher and mathematician Kurt Gödel, who had challenged Russell and Whitehead's argument. Gödel had actually been trying to prove the same point as the British pair. He believed there must be true statements about numbers that cannot be proved in their system, however, and which he said were therefore "undecidable."

Removing the Element of Doubt

Newman's lectures also discussed the work of the German mathematician David Hilbert. In 1900, Hilbert had compiled a list of some 23 problems that he thought needed to be solved in order to advance the study of mathematics beyond what he saw as its contemporary position. Some of those problems are still unsolved today. Hilbert thought that a set of instructions, or "algorithms," might be discovered that could be used to work out whether a statement were undecidable or not. If it could be found, he believed, mathematicians would be able to remove the undecidable statements from their calculations.

EXTENSION ACTIVITY

Video

Alan Turing—Celebrating the life of a genius

Examine Alan Turing's contribution to computer science and interpret his vision for computer technology and its function.

1. How did the "imaginary machine" of Turing work? What was its purpose? Why is it described as "one of the cornerstones of computer science"?
2. How does the use of computer technology in modern daily life differ from Turing's ideas of computer technology and its purposes? In what ways is this use similar? How is it different?

Weblink

Royal Pardon for Codebreaker Alan Turing

Review Alan Turing's relationship with the British government and its consequences on his research and work.

1. Why, despite his scientific achievements and contribution to the war effort, was Turing removed from his position? Would a removal for these reasons take place today? Why or why not?
2. For what reason did the British government issue an apology in 2009? Why might the British government have chosen to grant a posthumous pardon to Turing in 2013? Why might it have taken 61 years after Turing was condemned for this pardon to be granted? Justify your responses.

RUBRIC

Analyzing a Newspaper Article

Students will assess a newspaper article and write an analysis. An exemplary analysis will meet the following criteria.

- Identifies the topic of the article
- Identifies the main points and opinions presented in the article
- Identifies the writer of the article
- Presents information about the writer and infers how his or her life may have shaped this opinion
- Assesses the writer's reliability
- Analyzes how the writer makes his or her argument
- Uses evidence from the article to show how the writer supports his or her argument
- Analyzes the writer's use of literary devices to enhance the article
- Differentiates between the facts and opinions presented in the article
- Identifies when and where the article was published, and determines its intended audience
- Identifies and understands the goals of the article
- Assesses the effectiveness of the format in presenting the writer's argument
- Connects the article to the societal and historical context in which it was written
- Infers what is not said about this topic in the article
- Identifies what information is unintentionally implied in the article

Bletchley Park was a country house in central England. The codebreakers there were sworn to keep their work secret, even from their own families.

The Dream Machine

Turing began to study mathematical logic more deeply. He devised an imaginary "machine" to prove that a number of important mathematical problems could have no effective decision process. Turing thought of his machine as being made up of an infinitely long tape, divided into an infinite number of cells containing instructions, and a device that read these instructions. The machine would be able to calculate anything for which there was an algorithm. If the algorithm told it how to determine whether or not a number was prime, the machine would be able to do so. If the algorithm told the machine the rules of chess, the machine could play chess. There could be any number of these machines doing different tasks.

Turing then imagined a single machine that could interpret the instructions for all the individual tasks and so do everything the separate Turing machines could do. He named this a Universal Turing Machine (UTM). Scientists today understand that Turing had laid out the principles for a digital computer. The Turing machines can be seen as computer programs, and the UTM as the computer itself. Using his imaginary machine, Turing showed that there will always be undecidable problems in math.

While studying at Princeton University in the United States, Turing met the Hungarian-born mathematician Johann von Neumann. Neumann realized the practical possibilities of Turing's work. Back in England, Turing began building a mechanical device to carry out complex calculations. His work was halted when World War II started in 1939.

Breaking the Code

Soon after the war began, the British secret service set up the Ultra Project at Bletchley Park in central England. The project aimed to decode signals sent by the Germans. British radio operators intercepted hundreds of coded German military signals every day.

The signals were sent in code via a device called an Enigma machine. The Germans believed this code could not be broken, but the British were determined to break it. They knew that, if they could decipher the code, they would be able to pass on vital information about troop movements and bombing raids to the military planners.

An assortment of people was assembled at Bletchley Park. They included experts in languages, chess-players, crossword-puzzle solvers, and others thought to have the kind of brain needed to decipher coded messages. Soon Turing joined the top-secret project. One Bletchley Park worker recalls: "There was a great degree of tolerance at Bletchley for eccentricities. At least half of the people were absolutely mad. They were geniuses, no doubt many of them were extremely clever, but my goodness they were strange in ordinary life." Even in this company, Turing's behavior stood out, and he managed to upset many fellow workers. His pattern of working was also considered odd. He would stay up for days and nights on end and then fall asleep at his desk.

The Enigma machine was so complex that codebreakers needed to know the starting position of each of the machine's three rotors in order to decipher each message. There were billions of possible settings. Turing saw that, if solutions were to be found in time to help the war effort, the process would have to be mechanized. With some of his colleagues at Bletchley Park, Turing developed the "bombe," a form of computer that enabled many possible solutions to codes to be quickly substituted and checked. The first bombe was ready for use in 1940, but it proved rather slow in its calculations. This improved by late 1941, by which time there were 15 bombes on site. Unknown to the Germans, Enigma messages were now usually decoded within hours of being intercepted.

The Enigma machine had a set of rotors beneath a keyboard. The message had to be decoded on another machine with the same rotor settings.

EXTENSION ACTIVITY

More

Enigma Machines

Analyze the importance of codebreakers to decipher messages sent by Enigma machines.

1. How did Enigma machines work? How did codebreaking work? Explain the process in your own words.
2. Do you agree with Winston Churchill's statement? Why or why not?
3. Do you know any other technological or scientific advances that have been stimulated by war? Support your answer with examples.

Weblink

The Imitation Game: who were the real Bletchley Park codebreakers?

Examine the article from the July 2016 issue of *The Telegraph* about the codebreakers of Bletchley Park and their representation in modern media.

1. What did Winston Churchill mean by defining the group of Bletchley Park codebreakers as a "goose that laid the golden egg and never cackled"? Why would he order that records of their work be destroyed?
2. Besides Turing and his important role as codebreaker, what were the roles of the other members of the Bletchley Park group? In your opinion, would Turing's codebreaking work have had the same outcome without their contributions? Why or why not? Formulate some hypotheses.

RUBRIC

Write an Abstract

Students will use their library or *Google Scholar* to find a scientific research article or study related to the internet, then write a 300-word abstract. An exemplary abstract will meet the following criteria.

- States the research question or problem that the author is answering
- Indicates the significance of the issue
- Describes and explains methods used by the scientist(s)
- Explains why the methods used by the scientist(s) were appropriate
- Explains why this article or study stands out and how it is different from others
- Clearly states how the article or study advances knowledge about the topic, why it is important, and how it can be used
- Introductory statement is clear, concise, and engaging
- Purpose is clear, concise, and relevant
- Explanation of the findings includes what was expected, discovered, accomplished, collected, and produced
- Clearly states the conclusion
- Conclusion describes how the work contributes to the field
- Writing is appropriate and free from grammatical errors

From early 1942, however, German U-boats, or submarines, began to use a much more complicated code. This was the Lorenz cypher. It was not until March 1943 that the codebreakers found the key to deciphering it. In 1942, electronic technology helped to speed up decoding. Turing helped build the first all-electronic digital computing machine at Bletchley Park. The computer was known as Colossus. It began operating in late 1943.

Intelligent Machines

When the war ended in 1945, Turing took a post at the National Physical Laboratory in London, where he worked on the design of a new computer, the Automatic Computing Engine (ACE). In 1946, the first all-electronic, programmable digital computer was built at the University of Pennsylvania, Philadelphia. Meanwhile, Turing's project was hampered by a lack of government funding. He eventually decided to return to Cambridge, but in 1948, he was invited by Max Newman to move to Manchester University in northwest England, where Newman taught mathematics. There, Turing began work on the computer known as the Ferranti Mark I.

Two years later, Turing published "Computing Machinery and Intelligence," proposing that it would be possible to make computers appear to be thinking for themselves in ways that humans would. This is known as artificial intelligence. To test this theory, Turing devised what he called the Imitation Game, which later became known as the Turing Test. In the test, a questioner is positioned on one side of a screen, on the other side of which are a computer and a human. If the questioner cannot decide from each subject's answers which is which, then the computer can be said to be "thinking" as successfully as a human.

The British were able to decode messages sent on the German Lorenz machine after an operator made a mistake and sent two similar messages.

A Tragic End

In the 1950s, the Cold War was at its height. This was a period of extremely tense relations between the United States and its allies and the Soviet Union and its power bloc in Eastern Europe. The tension was marked by the rapid buildup of nuclear weapons on both sides. Turing went back to carrying out highly secret decoding work on behalf of the British government at this time. He still carried on his university research, and in 1951, was elected a member of the Royal Society in London.

Turing died of cyanide poisoning in 1954. He was said at the time to have accidentally contaminated his hands while conducting a chemical experiment. Some people now believe he may have killed himself after being questioned by the police. Turing was a homosexual, which was illegal in Great Britain at the time.

Many women worked at Bletchley Park. A few were codebreakers, but many more were secretaries or technicians who worked on the Colossus computer.

THE COMPUTER REVOLUTION

In Turing's day, computers were enormous machines. It seemed they could only get bigger as they became more powerful. That changed thanks to two technological advances, the transistor and the microchip. Transistors are small devices that can amplify electric currents as well as switching currents on and off. They enabled people to build computers that were more compact but also far more powerful. The microchip was invented in 1959. This tiny chip, measuring about 0.15 square inch (1 sq. cm), was made of silicon, a semiconducting material onto which miniature electric circuits could be etched. The early chips carried about 10 transistor circuits, but by 1969, 1,000 transistor circuits could be embedded on one chip. Eventually, scientists could embed hundreds of thousands of transistor circuits and other electronic components onto one microchip. The age of the desktop personal computer was born.

EXTENSION ACTIVITY

More

The Computer Age

Explore the origin of the internet.

1. Why was the internet invented? Do we use it for the same reasons today? Why or why not?
2. How did network communication systems change over time? Has their evolution had consequences outside the scientific and professional fields? Support your answer with examples.

First Hand

Letter from Alan Turing to W. Ross Ashby

Review the letter written by Alan Turing about the Automatic Computer Engine.

1. Who is the designated receiver of the letter? What is the tone of the letter? In what term does it describe the Automatic Computer Engine?
2. What was the purpose of a machine capable of reproducing "the activity of the brain"? Why might Turing have considered the "uncritical" nature of the Automatic Computer Engine to be a "disagreeable feature"? Do you agree with his assessment? Why or why not?

JONAS SALK

1914–1995

In 1955, U.S. microbiologist Jonas Salk developed the first **vaccine** against the infectious viral disease known as polio. This disease can affect the spinal cord and brain and cause paralysis. Salk went on to search for a vaccine against Acquired Immune Deficiency Syndrome (AIDS).

Jonas Salk was born in New York City on October 28, 1914, to Polish-Jewish immigrant parents. Salk graduated in medicine in 1934 and entered the New York University College of Medicine. There, he worked with the microbiologist Thomas Francis, Jr., carrying out research into the epidemiology of influenza. Epidemiology is the science concerned with the pattern and control of disease in a population. By 1940, Francis had isolated two distinct types of influenza **virus**.

Salk then worked at the Mount Sinai Hospital in New York City, but in 1942, he joined the Virus Research Unit headed by Francis at the University of Michigan School of Public Health. The unit had been set up by the U.S. Army to develop a vaccine against influenza. A vaccine gives **immunity** against a particular disease by stimulating the production of **antibodies** to destroy the **microorganisms** that cause it. Francis developed "killed-virus" vaccines against both types of influenza virus. With this type of vaccine, the virus is made inactive without completely destroying it. Vaccines are also given in "attenuated" form. This is when the virus or other microorganism is still alive, but its ability to cause infection has been weakened.

In 1947, Salk moved to the University of Pittsburgh, Pennsylvania. He took charge of a team that was conducting a program to investigate viral diseases. It was there, working in collaboration with the National Foundation for Infantile Paralysis, that Salk began working to develop a polio vaccine that would give people immunity against the disease.

Ancient Disease

Polio is an acute infectious disease with symptoms including fever, sore throat, and vomiting. In most cases, the patient makes a full recovery after an attack. About 20 percent of patients can suffer permanent paralysis and muscle loss, however. If the upper part of the spinal cord is infected, chest muscles may become paralyzed, affecting breathing. If the brain stem is affected, the patient loses the use of the muscles involved in swallowing and talking and may choke to death. In the 1940s, polio was still a greatly feared disease.

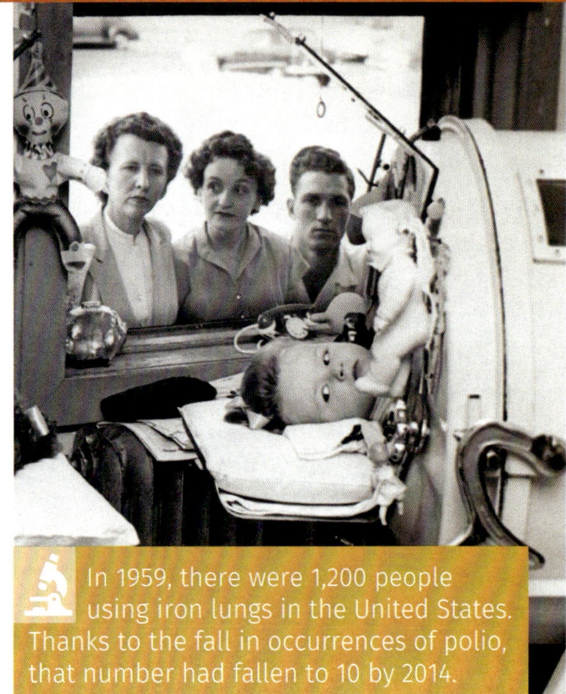

In 1959, there were 1,200 people using iron lungs in the United States. Thanks to the fall in occurrences of polio, that number had fallen to 10 by 2014.

Polio is believed to have occurred throughout history. A figure carved on a pillar in ancient Egypt between 1580 and 1350 BC may depict a polio victim. One of the most famous victims of polio was Franklin D. Roosevelt, four times president of the United States, who was stricken by the disease in 1921. In the mid-twentieth century, polio had reached epidemic levels in the United States. The disease was passed on at school or at swimming pools and other places where young people met, and thousands of new cases were reported each year. Many victims died. Others were left paralyzed, with wasted limbs. Some sufferers lost their respiratory muscles, so they could not breathe. Although the "iron lung," developed in 1932, kept them alive by forcing air in and out of their lungs, they had to spend their lives flat on their backs in bed. Massive efforts were directed toward finding a cure for the disease. The National Foundation for Infantile Paralysis was at the head of a huge publicity campaign to fight polio. It supported Salk's research.

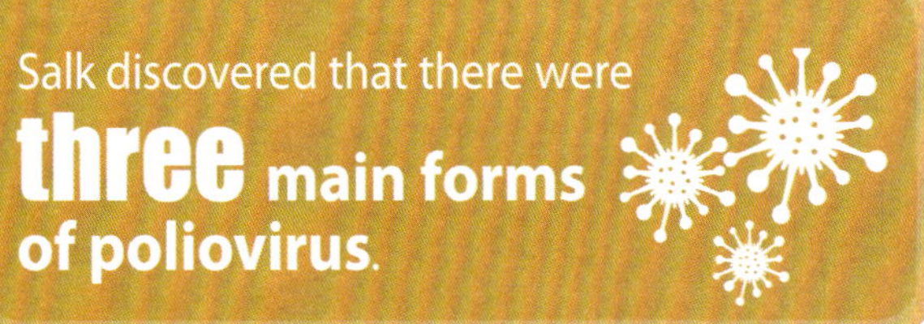

24,414
The number of **Americans killed or paralyzed by polio** in the epidemic of 1952

EXTENSION ACTIVITY

Video

The Iron Lung
Examine the technology behind the iron lung as shown in the video.

1. How does an iron lung work? Explain it in your own words. Why were they used in severe cases of polio?
2. Who created the machine? Why is it called an iron lung? What were the main improvements in the later models?
3. Research online or at the library to learn about further developments in this technology. How have these developments led to improvements in the lives of individuals affected by diseases or disabilities?

Weblink

Polio Virus and its odd history
Review the history of our understanding of the polio virus.

1. Why, if the polio virus was documented in ancient Egypt, did it become a major medical emergency only during the twentieth century? Why was it not recognized as a specific virus prior the late eighteenth century?
2. How did cleaner environments contribute to the spread of polio? What are the characteristics of the disease?
3. In your opinion, can polio be eradicated? Why or why not?

Search for a Vaccine

Polio is caused by a virus, which is a tiny microorganism too small to be seen except with the most powerful scanning electron microscope. Viruses cannot be grown in a test tube, as they can reproduce only inside living cells. In 1948, U.S. microbiologist John Enders and virologists Frederick Robbins and Thomas Weller found a way of growing viruses in tissue taken from chick embryos. They used the **antibiotic** penicillin to keep the material free from **bacterial** infection.

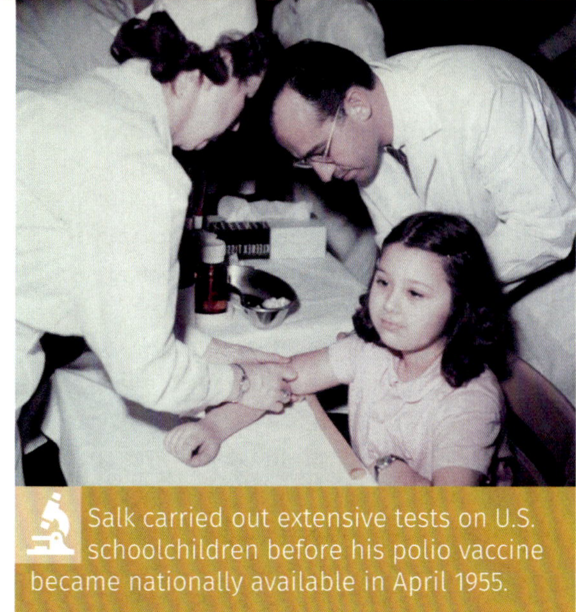

Salk carried out extensive tests on U.S. schoolchildren before his polio vaccine became nationally available in April 1955.

This was the breakthrough Salk needed. He took viruses from the spinal cords of polio victims and grew them in the new medium. Tests revealed that there are three types of poliovirus. By 1952, Salk had produced a killed-virus vaccine effective against all three.

After testing the vaccine in monkeys, Salk gave it to children who had recovered from polio. They had developed immunity, so they could not catch it again, but the quantity of virus-fighting antibodies in their blood increased. Salk tried it on himself, his wife and sons, and on other volunteers. Everyone injected with the vaccine produced antibodies against the three poliovirus types.

Polio was such a widely feared disease that people rushed to take advantage of the new vaccine.

The next step was a large clinical trial. This would require larger amounts of vaccine than Salk's laboratory could produce, so five drug companies were licensed to produce it. There were faults in some of the vaccine used. As a result, 204 people contracted polio and 11 died. Salk insisted that all further vaccines be tested by the public-health service, and no more accidents occurred.

In the clinical trials that began in 1954, 1.8 million U.S. schoolchildren received either the vaccine or a placebo, which is a harmless substitute. Results showed that the vaccine was safe and effective, and on April 12, 1955, a vast public **inoculation** campaign began. In 1952, there had been 58,000 new cases of polio in the United States. By 1962, the number had fallen to around only 1,000.

Killed-virus vaccines such as Salk's polio vaccine have a drawback over live-attenuated vaccines. They have to be administered in greater quantities and over a longer period. People had to receive two or three injections of Salk's vaccine several weeks apart, followed by booster doses six to twelve months later and in subsequent years. While Salk was testing his vaccine, Albert Sabin was completing his work on a live-attenuated vaccine, which could be given once only by mouth, often on a sugar lump. Once it passed its clinical trials, it replaced the Salk vaccine.

Recognition and Honor

Salk's conquest of the polio threat in the United States made him a national hero. Some of his colleagues felt their own contributions to the development of the vaccine were overlooked. In 1955, Salk was made a member of the French Legion of Honor.

In 1957, Salk was appointed professor of experimental medicine at Pittsburgh University, Pennsylvania. In 1963, he became director of the Institute for Biological Studies in San Diego, California. He also established the Salk Institute for Biological Studies in La Jolla. He later tried to develop vaccines against multiple sclerosis, a chronic disease of the central nervous system, and AIDS. Salk was awarded the Presidential Medal of Freedom in 1977. He died on June 23, 1995.

THE SUGAR-LUMP VACCINE

Soon after the trials of Salk's vaccine, another U.S. scientist, Albert Sabin, developed an alternative vaccine. He obtained permission from the Soviet authorities to test his vaccine in Russia. It was also tested in Eastern Europe and Great Britain, and from 1961, it was available in the United States. The Sabin vaccine is often given to children on a sugar lump. It causes an infection in a person's intestines, which triggers the forming of the antibodies to resist the polio virus. Like Salk, Sabin did not take out a patent on his vaccine, insisting that it be given free of charge. During the early 1960s, about 100 million European children and a similar number of Americans of all ages received the vaccine.

EXTENSION ACTIVITY

More

Albert Sabin

Examine the text describing how Albert Sabin contributed to the development of the polio vaccine.

1. How did Sabin's research differ from that of Salk's? Describe it using your own words.
2. Why might Sabin have used monkeys for his experiments on the polio vaccine? Formulate some hypotheses.

Document

Salk Says Test of Vaccine Show Halt of AIDS Infection in Chimps

Review the article in the June 9, 1989, issue of *The New York Times*.

1. In your opinion, why might AIDS have become a focus of Jonas Salk's research after his work on the polio vaccine? Formulate some hypotheses.
2. What was the significance of Salk's experimentation? Describe it in your own words. Why did Salk compare the stage of his experimentation reported in the article to the beginning of his work on polio vaccine?

RUBRIC

Creating a Timeline

Students will explore a topic related to a scientific event and create a timeline to present their research on scientific events connected to this topic. An exemplary timeline will meet the following criteria.

- Includes the most significant events pertaining to the topic to be compared and analyzed
- Includes interesting events
- Uses accurate information for all events, including date, location, and major details
- Orders the events in a chronological sequence
- Describes each event with accurate, vivid, and specific details
- Presents the topic from three or more perspectives
- Inspires the reader to ask thoughtful questions regarding the events and perspectives presented in the timeline
- Uses correct spelling, grammar, and punctuation
- Presents the timeline in a visually attractive and striking manner
- Presents the timeline in a neat, organized manner that is logical and easy to follow
- Uses creativity to present the timeline in an engaging manner
- Effectively communicates historical information relating to the topic
- Supports each event with reliable sources
- Includes a correctly formatted bibliography of all sources used to create the timeline

Timeline of Scientific Breakthroughs

The history of invention and engineering has been marked by important breakthroughs. Scientists have developed machines that harness forces such as heat or electricity to revolutionize work, transportation, and communications. They have also made great advances in combating serious diseases.

1764
James Watt makes existing steam engines more efficient by adding a separate condenser.

1837–1843
Charles Babbage begins to design an analytical engine, later hailed as the first computer. Ada Lovelace later proposed that the machine could be programmed using punch cards.

1876
Alexander Graham Bell files a patent for a telephone on the same day as another inventor, Elisha Gray from the United States.

1879
After many tests, Thomas Alva Edison uses a carbon filament to create the first light bulb for commercial sale.

1918
Fritz Haber wins the Nobel Prize for Chemistry for figuring out a way to artificially synthesize ammonia. Many people object to the award because of his role in developing poisonous gas.

1942–1943
As part of British attempts to break German wartime codes, Alan Turing builds the first electronic computer, Colossus, at Bletchley Park.

1955
The polio vaccine developed by Jonas Salk is launched in a national vaccination program.

2017
The World Health Organization says that polio has fallen by 99 percent around the world since the 1950s.

Quiz

1 What substances did Aristotle and the ancient Greeks think make up the four elements?

2 Which English engineer designed the steam engine James Watt was asked to repair in 1764?

3 How did Ada Lovelace suggest that Charles Babbage's analytical engine could be programmed?

4 Thomas Alva Edison's first successful invention was called a "stock ticker." What did the machine do?

5 Who was Edison's leading rival as a supplier of electricity in the United States?

6 How did Alexander Graham Bell first become interested in the mechanics of human speech?

7 In what family business did the German scientist Fritz Haber briefly work with his father?

8 What did Alan Turing call his test for figuring out whether a machine possessed artificial intelligence, or AI?

9 Which U.S. president of the 1930s was one of the most famous victims of the disease polio?

10 What are the two types of vaccine called, depending on whether they include living or dead microorganisms?

ANSWERS

1. Earth, water, air, and fire 2. Thomas Newcomen 3. With punched cards 4. It printed out changing prices on the Stock Exchange 5. George Westinghouse 6. By working with the hard of hearing 7. Selling natural dyes 8. The Imitation Game 9. Franklin D. Roosevelt 10. Live-attenuated or killed-virus vaccinations

EXTENSION ACTIVITY

Transparency–Timeline

Timeline of Scientific Breakthroughs

Analyze important events related to advancements in the fields of philosophy, invention, and engineering in different cultural, historical, and contemporary contexts.

1. Why might these events be featured in the timeline? What makes these events important or significant?
2. How might people from different social or ideological groups have interpreted these events when they took place? How might their opinions differ from those of people in the same social or ideological groups today? Why?
3. What effects did one of these scientific breakthroughs have on modern science?
4. How might these events have shaped the world today? Explain your response with evidence found on the internet or at the library.
5. How might recent events affect the way people interpret these past events?

Key Words

antibiotic: a substance that kills or prevents the growth of other microorganisms

antibodies: defense proteins made in the body to counter invading antigens

artificial intelligence: computer systems that can perform tasks that usually require human thought

astronomy: the study of the origin, motion, and makeup of material in the universe

atmospheric: relating to the atmosphere, the gaseous envelope around Earth

bacterial: related to single-celled microorganisms, or bacteria, that can carry disease

chemistry: the science concerned with elements and compounds, their makeup, and reactions between them

comet: a celestial body that travels around the Sun, usually in an elliptical orbit

condensed: changed from a gas or vapor to a liquid

eclipse: an event when one celestial body obscures the view of another

electric current: a flow of electrical charge through a conductor

electricity: the effect of charged particles at rest and in motion. Electricity provides a very adaptable form of energy.

energy: the capacity for doing work

force: the influence that changes a body from a state of rest to one of motion, or changes its rate of motion

immunity: the ability to resist infection by viruses, bacteria, and other microorganisms that cause disease

inoculation: the introduction of microorganisms or their products into living tissues in order to produce immunity

mathematics: the study of numbers, shapes, quantities, and space, and how they interrelate

microorganisms: tiny living organisms, such as any bacterium or virus

motion: movement, or the process of change in the position of one object relative to another

nitrogen: a gaseous element that forms almost 80 percent of Earth's atmosphere

Nobel prizes: prizes established with a bequest from the Swedish chemist Alfred Nobel

planets: any celestial bodies that orbit the Sun or other stars

rational: based on reason and logic

semiconductor: a material that can carry electrical current only under limited circumstances

stars: large, incandescent gaseous balls held together by their own gravity

vaccine: a substance that gives immunity against infectious disease caused by bacteria or viruses

virus: a tiny parasitic organism that reproduces only inside the cell of its host

Index

LIGHTBOX

SUPPLEMENTARY RESOURCES

Click on the plus icon found in the bottom left corner of each spread to open additional teacher resources.

- Download and print the book's quizzes and activities
- Access curriculum correlations
- Explore additional web applications that enhance the Lightbox experience

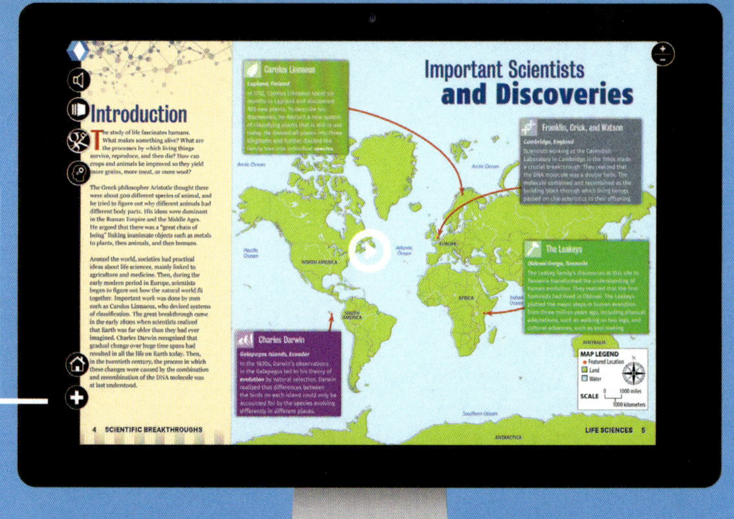

LIGHTBOX DIGITAL TITLES
Packed full of integrated media

VIDEOS

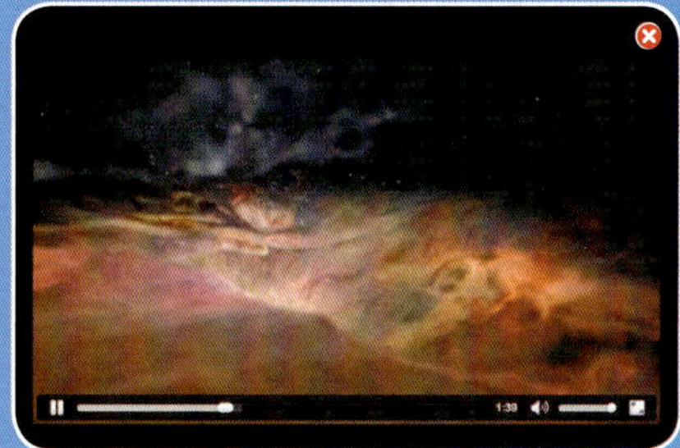

INTERACTIVE MAPS

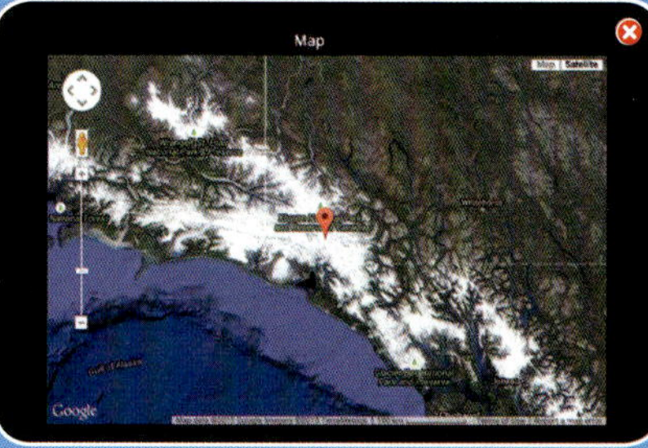

WEBLINKS

SLIDESHOWS

QUIZZES

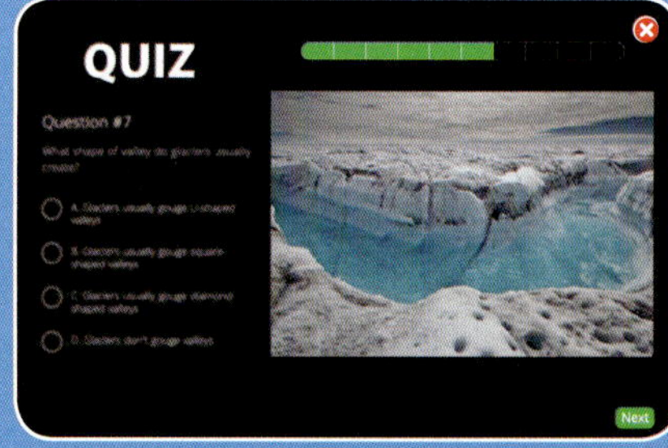

OPTIMIZED FOR

- ✓ TABLETS
- ✓ WHITEBOARDS
- ✓ COMPUTERS
- ✓ AND MUCH MORE!

Published by Smartbook Media Inc.
350 5th Avenue, 59th Floor New York, NY 10118
Website: www.openlightbox.com

Library of Congress Control Number: 2018937316

ISBN 978-1-5105-3761-3 (hardcover)
ISBN 978-1-5105-3762-0 (multi-user eBook)

Printed in Brainerd, Minnesota, United States
1 2 3 4 5 6 7 8 9 0 22 21 20 19 18

062018
121217

Project Coordinator: Jared Siemens
Designer: Ana María Vidal

Every reasonable effort has been made to trace ownership and to obtain permission to reprint copyright material. The publisher would be pleased to have any errors or omissions brought to its attention so that they may be corrected in subsequent printings. The publisher acknowledges Getty Images, Shutterstock, Newscom, and Alamy as its primary image suppliers for this title.